WHEN TO LET GO

A Christian Guide to

Letting Go

By:

GLADYS KEPNEY WHITE

First published March 2012

ISBN: 9780615586083

Printed in the United States of America

Cover illustration created by: Terri Crawford
Cover formatted by: Brittany McZeal

Scripture quotations are taken from the Hebrew/Greek Keyword Study Bible, unless otherwise indicated.

To: My Grandchildren

Timothy, Jayln, Josiah &

Journee

With Nana's Love

Acknowledgement

God,

The Author & Finisher of My Faith

TABLE OF CONTENTS

<u>FOREWORD</u>

Wife, mother, preacher, evangelist, and author – these are just a few of the titles of Gladys Kepney White. She wears many different hats, and she wears each well.

I have known Elder Gladys Kepney White since the time that her 2nd child, but 1st son at the age of three, was in my summer church music workshop for youth and young people called *Youth On the Winning Side.* This chance meeting (however, nothing happens by chance to Kingdom people) was the beginning of a long-lasting and continuing Christian association. Our bond has lasted throughout the years as a teacher of her sons in high school, as a mentor of her preacher/songwriter son, and as a fellow church member. Yes, we are both "transplants" in the same congregation-Nazaree Full Gospel Church!

When Elder Gladys approached me about reading her book before the final copy for the publisher, I didn't hesitate because of her proven way in presenting subject matter – printed and spoken. I knew that even if I didn't particularly like the book that I would find some "nuggets" of value for my Christian walk. However, as I read and flipped the pages, I was captivated by the information, the innovation, and the "just plain mother-wit" on each page of the book, made accessible by her successful "chunking" of the information in a manner to foster comprehension and retention.

Elder Gladys' approach is God-centered and the words on each page feel like *Rhema* in that most of the scenarios she presents are ones that we find daily, but the solutions and the conclusions that she offers are novel and thought-provoking AND all are supported by scripture.

The "birthing" process for *When To Let Go* may have taken more than 7 years; however, when readers pick up this book and read the information with open hearts and minds, the 13 chapters will be devoured within days. Additionally, if readers apply the information to their lives, effective change will be realized over the course of time as the Lord gives revelation.

The many titles that Gladys Kepney White wears are many. I want to add one more – FRIEND!

Yvonne Reed Matthews
Psalmist, Educator, Musician
Most of all – Friend

AUTHOR'S PREFACE

This book is all about releasing all to God; looking to Him who is the Author and Finisher of our faith. It took several years to complete this project. I had things and people who I held on to for dear life; only to discover that God demands our total allegiance. When there are situations that He knows should not be present in our lives, He warns us. We say that we love and trust Him, but yet we ignore warnings that could keep us safe and keep us in a growing relationship with Him. His love for us is enduring. He allows us time to get our acts together and to walk in His will, but we must let go of unhealthy baggage. We need to release those feelings, those emotions and even those people who are hindering our walk with God.

During the late summer of 2008, **FAVOR** Ministries, Inc. of which I am the founder, hosted a conference entitled, "*Release, Rejoice and*

Receive." Our guests were asked to write their issues, problems, etc., on small pieces of paper. We placed each piece of paper inside of an individual balloon. Early Friday morning, we took those balloons on to the beach where we had prayer and released the balloons in the atmosphere. We watched them until they flew out of sight. It was a breathtaking experience. Watching those balloons float away gave us all a sense of relief. It was as though some pressure had been taken off of our shoulders. It was good for the people. We received testimonies of prayers being answered before we left the conference. Just a simple act of faith changed lives and gave new hope. As long as we hold on to hurts and problems, we give Satan ammunition to use against us. We must let these things go by faith.

Releasing my father was the hardest task I have ever endured. He meant so much to me. His death was unexpected. It took my siblings and me by total surprise. Even though it was a shock for us, it was not for God. My brother and sisters discovered his body one Sunday in the apartment in which he lived. They called him several times that Saturday, but no answer. They decided to make a trip to Shreveport, Louisiana. Early Sunday morning, they drove to his apartment and found him. We do not know how long he had been there. I talked to him that Tuesday prior; one of the others talked to him Thursday, but there was no indication that anything was wrong. If he had only sneezed, coughed or complained, maybe we would have known to check on him sooner; but there was no warning. For a long time after the funeral, we beat up ourselves with guilt for not knowing. We could not let go of the thought that we should have called him daily. We should have made more trips home. We should have taken turns reminding him to take his medicine. We should have accompanied him on his doctor visits. We should have had someone else check on him. We were full of 'shoulda, woulda, coulda's.' His last words to me were, "Daddy loves you!"

I couldn't let him go. I cried daily. I cried in my car. I cried in my bedroom, my bathroom, my kitchen, all over my house. I cried at work. I cried at church. Months went by and just a thought of him and I would start crying. I never grieved over anyone who was so dear to me. In fact, I had never lost anyone who was so dear to me. I did not understand how long grieving was suppose to last. When will I stop crying? At one point, I thought about seeking professional help. Then it happened. One day I stopped crying. I don't know why, but I stopped. I was able to speak of him without breaking down. I knew he was safe with Jesus. Before, it was as though his spirit was still lingering and I was the one holding him up from a better place. I know he was in his destined place, but this is just how I felt. It was then I realized I had to let him go!

Letting him go did not mean forgetting him or all the wonderful interactions we shared. It did not mean disregarding his name. But it did mean I could move on with my life. When we hold on too tightly, we lose sight of the 'whole' of our lives. We are many components. Most of us have several hats to wear in the run of the day. We may be father, uncle, son and brother. We may be mother, daughter, sister and niece. If one component breaks down, we must be careful not to allow the others to go lacking. Holding on to grief, something I could not change, was causing me to fall short with other components of my life. Life does go on after death. I had to pull it together and let him go!

INTRODUCTION

I Corinthians 13:11 – "When I was a child, I spake as a child, I understood as a child, I thought as a child; but when I became a man, I put away childish things." Paul admonishes us to grow up. At some point in our lives, we should view life and all of its components in a more mature manner. "Eeny, meeny, miny, mo" should not be our technique for making a decision. A sense of maturity should be evident. Many scriptures speak to Christians being 'perfect.' Spiritual perfection is not doing things 100% correctly 365 days a year for all of your life. Spiritual perfection is changing the way we process sin and righteousness. If you are 50 years old, you should not be doing foolish things that you did when you were in your 20's or 30's. A level of maturity should be palpable in your relationships and your walk with God should be unspoiled.

I learned a difficult, but worthy poem from a dynamic minister, Bishop Abraham Wright, in my home town of Mobile, Al. Prayerfully I can remember it correctly. It went something like this:

Grow Up!

Grow Up!

Grow Up!

Grow Up!

Just what is the age of accountability? When do we become responsible for our actions? Is it 30, 40 or beyond that we can no longer point the finger at some one else or blame our mistakes on our age? When can we safely say that we have 'grown up?' Young is a good excuse, but the reality is that if death does not take us, we get older. Even in the court of law, ignorance is no excuse. If we failed to learn, the fault is considered ours. The age of accountability has changed for violent crimes. It was unheard of when I was growing up to try a child as an adult, but times have changed. We have subconsciously adopted the policy "if you are old enough to do the crime you are old enough to do the time!"

As long as we exist on earth, we have an opportunity to grow. There is always something we did not know; something else to be discovered or created. If we stop growing, we stop living. The problem comes with accepting the consequences of our learned or unlearned choices. Naturally, the older we are the better choices we make (or should make) because of experiences. This is maturity, or as the Bible will have it: perfection. Matthew 5:48

states "Be ye therefore perfect even as your Father which is in heaven is perfect." Here, Christ speaks of our growing up and making matured decisions. There comes a time when our childish thoughts, attitudes and conversations should come to an end. Our demeanor should be that of a matured Christian, no longer drinking milk, but digesting the meat of the Word!

GO WITH THE FLOW

If we remain open to change, we go through life a little better than we would if we resisted change. Going with the flow is easier than kicking against the prick. Just ask Paul! Near the Damascus Road, Christ confronted Saul about his badgering of Christian people. "I am Jesus whom thou persecutest: it is hard to for thee to kick against the pricks" (Acts 9:4). There, Saul experienced his transition from an enemy of Christ to an apostle of Christ. Paul humbled himself, accepted the change, walked in obedience and became one of the most prominent spokes' persons for Jesus Christ. Making this choice changed Paul's behavior. Through his walk with God, churches were established, pastors encouraged and people saved. All because he let go! We will go in more detail of Paul's life in another chapter.

If you do the same thing the same old way, you get the same results. However, the element of failure is present when change is involved. Failure is not a popular option with anyone. We have an inner drive and a need to succeed. If we make sudden changes, there is the possibility of failure. Change and growth come with success. You must be willing to do things a little differently and risk the results for the prospect of gain. Now, when situations turn out in the 'negative,' we find excuses or scapegoats to explain the reasons why. We hold on to the reasons and use them until we wear them thin. The reality is that if we never venture out and taste the 'sushi,' we will never know why it is so popular and why it is so successful! It is not until after we have explored a situation that we can make a constructive decision of whether we like it or not.

How do we let go? How do we step out on 'naked faith' and remain feeling secure? Letting go is not an easy task. We are comfortable in our safe, known environments. As long as we know what is expected to happen, we feel safe. When we can't predict the future, the sense of security is threatened. Yes, we fear the unknown. To counteract the fear, we buy insurance, though we believe God holds our future, just in case something happens. It is a safety mechanism; *modus operandi*, a safety technique. We invest in stocks, IRA's and 401k's to protect our future because we just don't know what will happen. We want a sense of financial, physical and emotional security.

It is the unknown that causes us to fear. Suppose I fail as a mother? Suppose my career never gets started, what then? Suppose he finds out that I'm not a virgin and suppose I find out he isn't who he says he is? How do we trust each other? This brings us back to 'choices.' There must be a handbook on making good healthy choices. Think about it. There is such a book!

It is critical that we make the choice to leave our safety net. We undertake the unfamiliar and try the unknown. If our parents are smart, they will change the lock on the door, leaving only the telephone to announce unexpected visits. Some young people are eager and ready to make the move, while others are skeptical and unsure. Both share a feeling of uneasiness whether it is shown or not. It is not until the move is actually made that the growing up process begins. Both child and parent must 'let go.'

Let It Go ....

Chapter I

CHOICES

Let it go.......

"In the beginning God created the heavens and the earth" (Genesis 1:1). "The grace of our Lord Jesus Christ be with you all. Amen" (Revelation 22:21). These are the first and last sentences of the Bible. A vast amount of information is concealed in and between the beginning and the end of the Holy Writ. Sixty-six books were written. Seven dispensations occurred and 8 covenants were made. Ten Commandments, 613 little laws of Moses and numerous other laws were issued, written and broken. Therein are both the creation of man and the fall of man. Processes of reconciliation were dispensed by God. The plan of salvation was explicitly given leaving no one amiss. All that was written was imparted to man by the inspiration of God for the edifying of the Body of Christ and the perfecting of the Saints. This information has been divinely inspired and translated by men. The Bible has been amplified, versified and simplified, and it is all inclusive. Everything you need and want to know about life is in the Bible. God fixed it to be just so. He knew that we would need examples, guidelines and most of all, structure.

From birth control to cloning, from multiple births to surrogate mothers, it is all enclosed in the Word of God. There is nothing new under the sun. To regulate our differences and to judge our temperament, God gave man standards. Without a standard being set, there would be no government. Standards must be in place to make the comparison and to formulate decisions of what is right and wrong. Thus, the dispensation of law entered the earth realm.

We broke the law. Christ came to fulfill the law; not to destroy it. "But we know that the law is good, if a man use it lawfully; knowing this, that the law is not made for a righteous man, but for the lawless and disobedient, for the ungodly and for sinners, for unholy and profane, for murderers of fathers and murderers of mothers, for manslayers, for whoremongers, for them that defile themselves with mankind, for menstealers, for liars, for perjured persons, and if there be any other thing that is contrary to sound doctrine" (I Timothy 1:8-10).

For the Christian, God in His infinite wisdom sets the standard. He is omniscient. He is absolute. He is immutable. He was in the beginning and He will be here through the end. John declares that,

"In the beginning was the Word and the Word was with God and the Word was God." Genesis declares that God spoke a word and the worlds were made manifest. When you have the ability to create, you automatically have the power to set standards for that which you have created. God is the Creator of everything and everybody! He has the right and the power to set the standard.

The standard we choose for our lives is entirely up to us. God has provided a rule book – the Bible, but the rules are not physically enforced. God allows each of us a will. He does not force His will upon us, but instead allows us to make decisions by our own will. However, the consequences of breaking the rules (laws) are administered by God. The choice is ours. Deuteronomy 30:15 - "See, I have set before thee this day life and good, and death and evil..."

We have a choice of being blessed or being cursed. It's our call! Our lives can be lives of peace (in Jesus) or lives of total chaos (outside of Jesus). "He came that we might have life and have that life more abundantly" (John 10:10b). We are the ones who get to decide upon lives of blessings or lives of cursing from the cradle to the grave. At a very young age, we learn that there are consequences to our actions. If we choose to disobey, we suffer the inevitable. If we choose to obey, we receive the more positive consequences. It is our prerogative. It is our choice.

YOU CHOOSE

When growing up as a small child, my brother was a hard one to convince that the stove was sometimes hot. Mama repeatedly warned him not to get too close to that stove. He was determined to see for himself. Finally, the day of truth arrived. Darrell touched the stove and found out for himself that it was just as Mama said: hot! And you thought experience was not a good teacher! Just like my brother, I am from Missouri (the show me state) by way of Shreveport, Louisiana. As a little girl, I was intrigued by the GE emblem placed in the middle of our large bladed fan. The GE was centered in the midst of huge black spokes. These spokes were open and exposed. I was determined to place my finger on the GE while the fan was in the 'on' position. Mama said, "You gonna cut your fingers messing with that fan!" I did not know how to live by faith nor Mama's good advice. I can do this and in spite of what Mama said, I will not get hurt. So, I tried it. The blades on the fan did not change because of my will power. The blades remained sharp. The fan cut three of my finger tips. I made the choice. It was a bloody and painful one. I suffered the consequences. Lesson learned. My father would always say, "Let a hint from the wise be sufficient." Got it Dad!

Accordingly, everything has a beginning and everything has an ending. Our task is to see where we fit in the dash. Our existence is marked by a Birth Day with a dash in the middle and then follows

22

the date of our demise. For example, your birth date and death date may read: Sunrise December 1971 – Sunset March 2023. You don't have any control over your birth date or your death date. Some choices you make may draw you to a closer end date, but the ultimate decision belongs to God. Have you ever thought about it, you really don't know when, where or even why you were born? You only know what you were told. You have no control over how old you are. What you do have control over is what happens while you are here, in the middle, somewhere in the dash between birth and death! I remember the lines to an old hymn generally song at funerals. It said, "Let the work I've done speak for me."

Now, there is a second birth that is strictly up to you. Jesus told Nicodemus in John 3:7 - "Marvel not that I said unto thee, ye must be born again." Not your neighbor, not your parent nor your sibling, but you must be born again. You must accept the Lord Jesus Christ as a personal Savior. This birth is one of the most crucial decisions you will ever make in your life. There is no time frame, no 1-2-3 steps toward making the decision. There is always an open invitation for salvation. You are not too old, too ugly, too sinful or too anything to come to God. The day of your salvation is your God-given right and is absolutely your decision! It is a date that you will definitely remember. Isaiah said it was in the year that King Uzziah died that he first saw the Lord high and lifted up. Jeremiah said it was unto the end of the eleventh year of Zedekiah, unto the carrying away of Jerusalem captive in the fifth month that the Word of the Lord came unto him. Ezekiel said it came to pass in the thirtieth year, in the fourth month, in the fifth day of the month that the heavens were opened, and he saw visions of God. It was one Thursday night at the tender age of 17 that God spoke to my heart and I dedicated my life to him! It was a good choice that I have never regretted!

We were not responsible for what happened before we got here; nor will we be completely responsible for what happens when we leave. (I say completely because the legacy we leave whether positive or negative could very well affect the lives of our offspring.) We are, however, held accountable for what is done in the middle; in the dash! Upon the return of Christ, judgment is inevitable; but, it will be different for the Saints than for the Sinners. Sinners will be judged for what they do best: sin! Saints will be judged for their works of love.

The dash consists of a culmination of choices. Life is all about choices. We sometimes make good ones and we sometimes make bad ones. What we need is guidance. New moms have no rule book on how to be successful mothers. Sure, they can read Doctor Spock. But the real test is when there is a crisis and they can't find the book, or something comes up that is not covered in the book. What a good time to depend on the wisdom that comes only from God! There are so many questions. "What do I do when no one is around? What do I do when I can't find the book? Upon whom do

24

I depend? Is there anyone available to help me make good, sound decisions?" God has given each Christian a communication line to heaven. It is called prayer. He has given us a guide to channel us through the uncertainties of life. He is called the Holy Ghost. Prayer is the means of getting in touch with the Holy Ghost who can best utter our issues to God the Father.

During Moses' time, God instituted a dispensation of government. God handed down laws and restrictions to be adhered to for better living. Before this, man did what ever was right in his own eyes. Exodus covered every wayward act that could have been conceived. Laws were given that showed man how to treat his neighbor: laws of human relations and laws against violence. There were laws of how to worship our creator and laws of who would be in charge of that worship. Specific construction plans for the temple were given to Moses as to how God wanted His sanctuary built for that worship. Feast days were declared and regulations for the Sabbath. God issued the 'Order of Service' that he wanted for the people who would be called by His name. God fixed it so that the people could be cleansed of their sins and come before a most Holy God to worship Him in spirit and in truth!

Moses' third book, Leviticus, picks up after Exodus with more laws. In Leviticus, we find laws of what to eat and what not to eat. Purification laws were set for women after childbirth and for the cleansing of lepers. Forbidden sexual practices were named. Rules for burnt meat and sin offerings were given that the people may be purified before God. Instructions of peace offerings were given for the showing of thanksgiving. God left no stone unturned. There were laws of holiness and justice. He even gave us a penalty for sin. Man's responsibility was to keep the law, and to love and please God. Being the merciful God that He is, He also established a day of atonement. Atonement was the penitence we needed to maintain a relationship with God. He knew that we would sin and come short of His glory. It was our nature. It was His mercy in action. Thank God for mercy.

We serve a sovereign God. He knew that we would fail even with our most sincere efforts to keep the law. So, He devised diverse ways of reconciliation. He gave us kings, and prophets and judges. He knew if there were no laws we would never grow to maturity and live a wholesome existence. This is where the only thing that He has allowed us to own (or have complete charge of) comes into play. He gave us a will. It is up to us to make the choice to do good or to do evil. Our will is our inner desire that we actually put into practice. It is that thing that we want to do whether it is the right thing to do or not. It is essential that we strive to make our will line up with the will of God. When His will becomes our will then we are walking righteously before Him. The safest place in the whole wide world is in the will of God.

This is all a part of the growing up process. We must leave all of the people who guided us through life and helped us to make sound practical decisions. We must let go of the dependency shared with mother and father. What do we do when there is no one there to remind us of the little things like laundry, paying bills or getting gas for the car? Funny thing, as long as we are under 30 years of age, our mistakes are excused because of our youth. Statements are made like, "Oh, he is just young, that's why he did it; or she's just a child." Once we have made it to the '30 Hill' (that's 30 years old of course), the statement changes to, "Now, she is old enough to know better."

All of the lessons that our parents taught us have significance when we are of age. Before, we thought that it did not matter what 'they' said because we were insistent on having things done our way. And then the real world happened! We became 'they'. Now as adults, we are left alone to make crucial decisions that will make or break us. No one is there to say go left or go right. It is up to us. We decide using the skills and wisdom that has been passed on to us. Our decisions lead to our success, or sometime, to our failure.

Bad Decisions: Let them go!

Chapter II

PARENTS

Let it go.......

True parenting deserves a Bachelor of Arts degree, Bachelor of Science degree, a doctorate and/or a Nobel Peace Prize. It is unquestionably "on-the-job" training. The pay is seldom monetary, but usually rewarding. When you, as a parent, see a well-rounded individual, who is not void of mistakes, but able to rise up from them, you have completed and successfully passed a course in parenting. When you have a young adult that is capable of finding his or her own solutions, standing independently and making decisions that will be beneficial to the physical, spiritual and emotional growth, you can take a bow.

Our first child graduated from Southern University, Baton Rouge, Louisiana, in 1997. Before the graduation ceremony, Eboni sternly requested that I not shout, scream or throw balloons when she crossed the stage to receive her degree. She felt this would make the people think that she had a difficult time getting through school. I did not care what they thought and I did not agree to behave. This was a milestone in both our lives and I was happy! She was about to embark upon her future and her father and I were responsible for giving her a good jump start. So, I was one grateful mother. My husband and I had one down and two to go. There was no containing my jubilance. To our surprise, the chancellor actually asked all the parents to stand and to take bow for a job well done.

It is the parent's job not to be an enabler of detrimental behavior or of needy people, but rather to build strong personalities that can brave life's storms with the assurance of inward personal power. This involves tough love, undesirable restrictions, looking the other way and not rushing in to fix things and situations that can be solved with time and a little common sense. Sometimes we have to take a step back and analyze the situation to realize it will not kill them if we step aside and allow them to grow a little. It may take them a little extra time to come up with the same solution, but experience is a good teacher. It is not the best teacher, but it remains a good one. Experience allows us to feel, to interpret and to conclude with our own personal faculties. I can tell you that a doughnut is sweet, but it is better when you taste it. The parent warns of impending danger and just sometimes the child listens and sometimes, unfortunately, he doesn't. If we permit that child to suffer some of the consequences of life, he becomes a stronger adult than ones who have only assimilated experiences. There comes a time when we must allow our teachings to be exercised. We have to let go.

The question becomes, "When should the child be released from dependency?" When does the parent know that the child is ready? The answer is that the parent will never know. Life is full of trials and errors. When it was time for me to make a decision of what college I would attend, a controversy arose in the Kepney household. My father wanted me to attend school at home. I wanted to go away. My mother thought I should go where ever I wanted to go. Dad suggested that I was not ready to leave home. I thought I was ready to leave home. My mother stated that she was ready for me to leave home. Imagine that!

The final analysis was that I would do better in the place of my choice than a place where I was forced to go. I was allowed to leave – a good choice. I could not pay for the experiences that I had on that campus nor the lessons that I learned from the extra-curricular activities. My parents had poured into me for 17 years. It was now time to test the waters. It was time to make applicable all that I had received from my parents. Was I ready? No.

-Parents-

Travel back in time with me. Here I was in a school some 400 miles away from home. There were no cell phones in 1971. I did not own a car. I had no kitchen at my immediate disposal. I had no bedroom of my own. I had to share a living room and bathroom. I had to catch the bus to go downtown. The conveniences of home vanished. Was I ready? The first semester as a freshman will cause a person to grow up or to break down. Statistics state that more young people quit college in the first semester than any other when they are away from home.

My parents had done their part. They secured me financially. They bandaged my cuts and bruises. They nurtured my character and groomed my personality. They had given me Jesus and all that they knew about the Word of God. They made sure that I went to elementary and high school. They kept up with my grades to make sure I passed the test so I could further my education. They dressed, fed and loved me. What more could they do? It was now time for them to let go of me - their eldest child. Some children, maybe I should say young adults, never leave home. It is not because they are not ready, but rather because of their fear of the unknown. When the choice becomes leaving the comforts of home to venture into an unknown scenario, the unwilling children will stay. It is up to the parent to deliver the ultimatum. The parent must give the push to make the change.

Eagles are ideal examples of good parenting. The eaglets are fed by their mother from beak to beak until she feels that they are ready to go out on their own. She hunts for the food and delivers it to her young. When the mother eagle knows that her babies have been strengthened with enough nourishment, she takes them from the nest for a trial run. She drops them without notice. Of course their first flight is a disaster, but she allows them to plunge downward just a little bit before rescuing them from the fall. She repeats the drop. The eaglet struggles. The next time she allows the eaglet to fall a little further, but each time she is there to sweep it up before hitting the ground. After this is done a few times, the eaglet realizes that it must do something to save itself. (What a revelation!) The mother eagle drops it again. This time the eaglet uses what it has, what it knows, what it has experienced and what it has been taught by its mother to fly. This procedure is done repeatedly until the eaglet's wings are adjusted to the wind factor and it is able to fly on its own. Parents are to help children adjust, but the parents should not make the adjustment. We must all discover our personal niche.

The most significant component in this process is that the eaglet realizes that it must do something for itself. While living with my parents, I never concerned myself with the payment of the utility bills, the house note nor the purchasing of food for the family. I just lived, slept and ate there. It was not until I was on my own that I figured out that these things were a part of life. My College experience taught me to be responsible for my own clothes being cleaned, getting to the dining hall before it closed and going to class to learn what was necessary to pass the test. There was no personal coach to remind me of my responsibilities. There was no mother there to pick up behind me, to wash, to fold and put up my clothes. I was actually on my own. College is a good preparatory for life. There was no one there to encourage me to go to the library or to stay up a little later to complete the assignment. The professors did not act like personal guides. They gave the assignment and it was strictly up to me to carry it out. I had to step up to the plate.

If parents never teach responsibility, they will have children that will never desire to leave the nest. Preparation for adulthood starts with personal accountability. Parents give their children household chores in an effort to teach them to be responsible people. It is a good life lesson. We should teach children everything comes with a cost. Nothing is free. If you don't work you don't get paid. Paul said in II Thessalonians 3:10, "...if any would not work, neither should he eat." Amen! Mr. William Kepney worked for Texas Eastern Oil Company for over 30 years. When I was home for the summer between semesters in college, I worked for the same company at the same place as my dad. He charged me $5 a week for gas. In 1972, this practically filled up your car with gas being 44 cents a gallon. He made me pay him. He also required that I save my money for school to help defray the cost. I hated it, but it was a good lesson in responsibility. I learned that I would have to make wise decisions with my funds because I had costly responsibilities.

Allowance in our home was a gift. It was never up for debate. The parents decided the amount and how often we would receive. We did not get an opportunity to vote on the chore assignment nor the pay. The chore was mandatory whether you were compensated or not. It was our home and everybody had household tasks in it. Your guaranteed pay was the right to have at least three meals each day and sleep there in shelter without the threat of having to move out in the morning. The allowance taught you how to handle money. You had to budget and to save to get the item you longed to have in your immediate possession even if it took three or four allowances.

Often there was some 'overtime' which allowed for some extra cash. You could do an unpleasant chore for additional cash. It was highly inspected and paid according to the perfection of the work. This taught us merit. If we wanted to be paid well, we had to work well. One of the greatest commercials I have seen for young people demonstrated the importance of working well. It claimed that we should do work as if we had to sign our name to it.

As teenagers, we were constantly thinking about what we would do once we were grown and out of our parents' home. We could not wait to leave. It may have taken me a year after I was on my own before I realized just how good I had it at home. Newborns are carried in a baby seat or pushed in a stroller. They are fed, bathed, dried and clothed. Newborns have no car payments, power or water bills. They are free! They don't even have a laundry bill! Now, I am accountable for the rent, the utility payments, furniture and water bill. No one else is going to pay them. It is up to me. The keys that are in my purse are the keys to my house where my name is on the bills. My parents had their bills and now I have mine. I want my parents back!

The transition from child to adult is a huge dash in our time line. Often it is a difficult adjustment period not only for the child, but for the parent as well. What was once controlled is now slipping away. Parental control is only a temporary privilege. If used wisely, the off-spring will be prepared to face life challenges. Parents must be careful not to hold the reign too tightly. It is obvious that this is done with much resistance. We want to protect and nurture whenever possible. We realize that there comes a time when we must let go, but when? Tough love has to be exercised or a child will never grow to maturity. Gradual pulling of the apron string can help ease us into the transition. Parents must learn this phrase: 'You figure it out.' Just like the eaglet, the child will learn to fly.

With all that my parents taught me, the best lesson was to trust in God. When I could not reach them, I could always reach Him. He is only a prayer away. God is Jehovah Shammah. He is the God that is present: always near. God is omnipresent. He is every where. He has the awesome ability to be in all places at the same time. The God that my mother bragged about was with her and with me as well some four hundred miles away. Times would get hard and it appeared no relief in sight, but I knew God was there! He was now my leaning post that never fell; that never left or allowed me to feel alone. I learned that with God all things were possible and that I could do all things through Christ who strengthened me! My parents learned to trust the God in me and we both learned to let go!

Parents: Let the Children go!

■■■■■■■■

Chapter III

CHILDREN

Let them go....................

A common aphorism is the saying, "possession is nine tenths of the law." I agree. If it is in my custody, living in my home, drinking my water, eating my food and sleeping in my bed, I am under the strong impression that it belongs to me. It is in my possession. It was probably given to me as a gift, or I purchased it or birthed it; either way, it belongs to me. It is furthermore under my covering, therefore subject to my rules and regulations. The most liberal parents have set guidelines for their possessions - human and material. In any model of life, where there is no government there is chaos. There is confusion. God is not the author of confusion (I Corinthians 14:33). The parent or parents are responsible for the contents of the home and the care of the same. Peace is the responsibility of the owners; in this case, the parents. Non-owners are subject to the owners. God is a god of order and orders come down; they do not go up!

"Children are a blessing from the Lord and blessed is the man that has his quiver full of them" (Psalm 127:5). Mandatory responsibility is issued with every child that is born. Somebody is responsible for the well being, the education and nurturing of that child. The operative word here is "child." The parent is responsible for the care of the child. My mother always exclaimed that when you begin to do what grown folk do, you are no longer a child. It was therefore your time to get your toothpick, your coat, your hat and leave her premises: a valid point. Grown folk paid bills, bought gas and had credit in their own names. They were expected to live on their own! If you remained under her roof, you were expected to live by her rules, no matter how old you got. The same rules that applied when you were a child, applied when you reached adulthood. If you were my mother's offspring, you were never "too grown" to abide by the household rules; nor were you too grown to receive corporal punishment. Mama always told us, "You may have grown taller, but I will always be bigger."

When we dropped off my oldest child at her college of choice, I had my first experience of letting a child go. She had decided to attend the same institution from which her father and I graduated some 20 Years ago, when we received her room assignment and went to the dormitory, we found out that she was not only in the same housing building in which I had lived, but she was on the same 3rd floor and even the same dorm mother was still there. Wow! After transporting all of her things to her room and saying our goodbyes, I could not leave. I sat on her bed and reminded her of college safety rules over and over again. My husband stood at the door beckoning me to come on and leave. I had all of the flash backs of what I had done on that 3rd floor, in that dorm and on that campus. I did not want her to have the bad experiences I had faced nor did I want her to experience some of the good ones (the ones that I thought were good, but really were not)! I had to let go. She was of age. It was now time for her to practice all of that which her father and I had taught her. It was time for her to make her own decisions and choices. I could no longer make them for her. I had to let go.

CHILDREN OF GOD

Let's take a look at it spiritually as children of God. Our Father knows when it is time to let us go. We attend church school, Sunday morning worship services and even Wednesday night services for years. If what we have heard, received and learned is never put into practice, we will never develop the long lasting relationship that God requires. Our spiritual muscles are strengthened when we exercise what we learn through faith. According to *James 2:26,* faith without works is dead: "For as the body without the spirit is dead, so faith without works is dead also." Faith on a shelf or just spoken is not beneficial. If we never exercise what we believe, we will become spiritually stagnated. Through His permissive will, God will allow trouble to come our way knowing that He has equipped us with what we need to fight the wiles of the devil. Our responsibility becomes merely having faith in what God has said. Job, a good example, was an upright man, but God allowed the enemy to reap havoc in his life for a season. Job's answer was "Though he slay me, yet will I trust in Him..." *Job 13:15a.*

The next time I had to let go of a child, my elder son was going off to a different college that was even further away. It was a tad easier than the first; however, it was still difficult because I wanted him to still need me. All of the difficult growing up years now seemed not so bad. I could remember saying, "I'll be glad when you grow up and get out of my house." Now, I wanted to take it back. I wanted to hold on to him. I wanted to hold on to the fact that without me, he would not be able to handle life's tortures. I wanted to remain the nurturing mom. I wanted to wipe away the tears and soothe the aches and pains. I wanted to be called on when he fell and scrapped his knee. I didn't want him to meet some other woman who could give him more than me and could help make decisions for him. I wanted to remain mother and best friend. How dare he grow up and not need me!

What are we to do? Parenting is the one job that takes us years to learn how to manage, somewhat successfully, and then appears to come to an abrupt end. One day they're seven and the next day they're seventeen. Where do the years go? After all it was just yesterday that I was pricing diapers. Just when my husband and I thought we were getting it right, it was just about over. The child is graduating and embarking on a career of his own. He is going to make his own decisions without me. Some other person is now going to do the comforting and the sharing. I spent 24 hours a day for the past 18 years, often times on my knees praying, making decisions for him. How am I going to spend my time now? This is why it is so very important that as we help to develop lives for our children that we not neglect our own. When the day comes that they remove themselves from our control, we must have lived a life that leaves us fulfilled and that is still in conquest of our own special interests.

Abraham had to let go of his first born son – Ishmael. In the 15th chapter of Genesis, God amended the covenant he made with Abraham. God promised him that his heir would come from his own bowels. "And he believed in the Lord and he counted it to him for righteousness" (Genesis 15:6). Even though Abraham believed God, he did not wait for the fulfillment of the promise. This prophecy did not take place immediately or soon enough for Sarah. She convinced Abraham to help God fulfill His Word. God does not need our limited finite help. Trusting and believing Him means also believing in His timing. We must hold fast to the promises of God and wait on the manifestation of the same. God knows what, when and how to handle any situation. He certainly knows when we are ready for the promises that He issues.

So, Sarah, Abraham's wife, took matters into her own hands. Instead of waiting on God, the couple decided to help God out and handle the situation. Sarah offers her handmaid, Hagar, to Abraham to start the conception process and the fulfilling of the promise. Abraham agrees. (Imagine a man agreeing to that!) Consequently, civilization has the first surrogate parent. This was the beginning of trouble. Anytime we try to fix God's promises to match our timing, we set ourselves up for failure. The consequence of acquiring a surrogate mother did not work. God had made the promise to Abraham that he would have a son and that he would be the father of many nations and God was capable of keeping His word. That should have been enough for them to patiently wait.

When Hagar conceived, she and Sarah ended up despising one another. This was not God's plan. Sarah treated Hagar cruelly, causing Hagar to decide to leave the camp. But she had to return. God sent an angel to speak with Hagar. She was still Sarah's handmaid and under the covering of Abraham and Sarah. It was and still is unlawful to be uncovered. God made a promise to Hagar that she would bare a son and she was to call his name Ishmael. "And God said unto Abraham, let it not be grievous in thy sight because of the lad, and because of thy bondwoman; in all that Sarah hath said unto thee, hearken unto her voice for in Isaac shall thy seed be called. And also of the son of the bondwoman will I make a nation, because he is thy seed" (Genesis 21:12 & 13).

Not only was there conflict with the two women, but after Sarah conceived and bore Isaac another conflict arose between the two boys Ishmael - the firstborn of Hagar, and Isaac - the firstborn Sarah. Ishmael may have known that he was actually his father's firstborn and the tradition was that the blessing of the father be given to the firstborn son. He may have also known that he was not going to be treated in that respect because he was not the first born of his father's wife, but of her handmaid. The scripture says that Ishmael began to tease Isaac and Sarah did not like it. She requested that Abraham rid the camp of Hagar and her son. Her allegation was that the heir should not grow up around the commoners. Abraham had to make a decision. How could he let go of his son? Regardless of how Ishmael was conceived, he was still the flesh and blood of Abraham.

How did I let go of my son? God intervened. How did Abraham let go of his son? God intervened. God let Abraham know that He had made a promise and that He would certainly keep all that He has promised. "And I will make a nation of the son of the bondwoman also, because he is your offspring" (Amplified Genesis 21:13). As difficult as it may seem or as long as it takes, we must hold on to the fact that God is true to His word. If we bring up our children under the admonition of the Lord, when they are old they will not steer from the truth of the Word. We can let them go when we know that we have given them all that we can and the best that we know. I submit to you that the best guarantee in life that we can give our children is "to know God."

One Saturday morning after all of my children were out of the house - one in college and the other two living on their own, I discovered a wonderful reality. Even though they had been collectively gone for more than a year, it just hit me all at once that I was home alone. I mean, really home alone. There was no baseball game or practice, no Easter play practice or Christmas practice, no little sticky hand children's birthday party, no project, and no homework. There was nobody to tend to but myself. I could do whatever I wanted to do. I was F R E E! I had arrived! Finally, after 34 years of nurturing, I had time for myself, but with no regrets. It was our pleasure to turn out young adults that my husband and I had prepared for the world!

When our children leave the nest, we have to make an assessment of our own lives. We can decide to be miserable because we are no longer in charge. We can choose to worry about them constantly. Or we can choose to go on with our lives, put them in God's hand and allow them to continue to grow. To grow means learning some things by experience. Sure, they are apt to make gigantic mistakes, but didn't we? Mistakes are 'miss' 'takes.' In other words, 'miss' 'takes' are times when we miss the goal and hit the post. We take the most difficult route or the longest route. The children of Israel made an 11 day trip into a 40 year journey because of their miss takes! They mistook God for one of the small gods that the Egyptians were serving and missed the crucial turning point of God's path for their lives.

PARENTS MUST LIVE THEIR LIVES

So, what do we do? Number one, we must program ourselves to live before our children leave the nest. My husband and I made sure that we enjoyed activities with our children, with each other and away from our children. We knew that we could not be with them 24/7. They had to learn to live with us and without us. Field trips were shared when they were young, but as they grew older, they were allowed to go without us. Quite naturally we did things together as a family, but none of us were denied some solitary time. I went to conferences out of state. My husband went on trips with his friends. My children were allowed to travel on school or church excursions without us. We all went to church, to family functions, reunions and the sort together. No one suffered because of this plan; instead, we all learned how to enjoy life with each other and sometimes apart from each other. We had no regrets.

Allowing our children to manage their lives, to some extent, without us prepared them for life on a college campus after graduating high school. Being fairly responsible for themselves helped them to adjust to campus life. They did not fall apart when something did not go their way or when they ran out of money. (They simply called home.) They knew that they had to make responsible decisions with their money and with their time. There was no one looking over their shoulders to remind them that they had to get up early or that they had no more clean underwear and it was time to do some laundry. Mama was not there to take them to McDonald's; so they had to make it to the cafeteria before it closed. Daddy was not there to fill the car with gas; so they had better save money for the fill-up! Push came to shove and it was time to grow up.

Fortunately, out of the three of them, we never received any frantic emergency calls. Like any college student, money got low and sometimes out. This was to be expected. As parents, we were so grateful that our children knew how to live without us. We taught them to trust God and to occasionally lean on us. We had done our part. We had three well-adjusted young people, bound to make human errors, but with strong enough personalities to take on the fierce courses of life.

The adjustment was more on our part than theirs. We had to learn to live with just each other. It was funny. Now we had to answer the phone ourselves. We had to get our own water. We had run to the store ourselves for the small items we forgot. We had to do the dishes! No children! We had to split the chores. Oh my! James had to cut the grass. I had to clean the kitchen. Oh my! Why did we let them go? Our youngest made the comment to me one day when he was still at home that our next house should be a flat – one story edifice. I told him that I prefer a two-story home. I like it; but when he is grown and gone, he can purchase a flat for himself and his family. He said, "Oh no, I'm getting a two-story home so that I can run my children up and down the stairs like you and daddy run me." I miss that!

Letting children go is more than just physical. We must let them go mentally and spiritually. The only possible way to be able to handle that is to prepare them before the time comes. Preparation includes giving them responsibilities and consequences of not meeting those assignments. If we allow our children to get away with slacking on their given responsibilities (such as chores around the house) then we will rear trifling adults. If we never give them any training on how to handle money, we will rear children who will always be dependent upon another adult's pocketbook, generally ours. If you never teach them to tithe, they will grow up giving grudgingly to the church which will cause them to miss out on God's blessings for their lives. "Bring ye all the tithes into the storehouse, *that there may be meat in mine house, and prove me now herewith, saith the Lord of hosts, if I will not open you the windows of heaven and pour you out a blessing that there shall not be room enough to receive it"* (Malachi 3:10).

49

-Children-

As parents, it is our duty to give our children everything we know, so when the transition time comes they will be ready and so will we. We must let them go!

Children: Let the parents go!

Chapter IV

RELATIONSHIPS

Let them go.......

Relationships come in many different forms. The Bible demonstrates relationships between married people, friends, and families. There are spousal relationships like Adam and Eve, and Priscilla and Aquilla. There are close friendships like David and Jonathan. There are in-laws who were bonded by circumstances like Ruth and Naomi; cousins like Esther and Mordacai, Elizabeth and Mary. There are mentors and mentees as Elijah was to Elisha. All relationships in the Bible are not good. Abigail was a good wife, but her mate, Nabal, was described as a churlish husband; his very name meant 'fool.' Saul was the hunter and David was the hunted. Notorious of them all was Judas, the traitor, and Jesus the Savior.

The mere fact that God demonstrates all of these unions in His Word lets us know that forming relationships is an important element to mankind. He expects us to form relationships with each other. Some of the relationships are for a lifetime whereas others are not. We must decipher which ones to cherish and to maintain, and when it is time to let go of others.

Christ gave us good examples of positive relationships which He experienced on earth. He chose 12 disciples to walk with Him on his earthly journey. He chose Peter, James and John to be close knit friends on His way to the cross. At Calvary, He reemphasized the importance of family and friends when he chose John to watch over his mother, and his mother to take care of his friend, John. Yet, God still allowed one who was "up to no good" to abide in the midst of Him and the disciples. Though he was deceitful, Judas developed relationships with Christ and the other disciples. If we are to take a lesson from this it would be that relationships are good; however, always be aware that the enemy can use those who are among us, but not with us. Only God knows the heart of a man. All those who claim to walk with Jesus may not have the Kingdom of God at heart. It is in the heart where relationships began to thrive and prosper; but, it is also in the heart where deceit and wickedness are birthed.

The 'heart', in this scenario, is not the organ behind the rib cage that is used to pump blood throughout the body, but rather, it is the mind where our thoughts are processed. "As a man thinketh in his heart, so is he" (Proverbs 23:7). "Out of the heart come the issues of life" (Proverbs 4:23). We do not think with the heart muscle. We think with our minds. It is in the mind where we decide to do right or wrong. It is here that choices are received and decisions are made. As we think, we do. Before you sin, you think about it. Many of our mistakes are made after we have mulled over the idea, but we end up making bad choices. This is why Paul encourages us to be not conformed to this world but to be transformed by the renewing of our minds. This is where change takes place. We must change our minds!

SEASONS

Most relationships are for seasons. Not all friends are bosom buddies for life or remain a BFF (best friends forever) connection. Some relationships are to test you, some to encourage you, some to make you think and some just to be there for you at specific times. When the person who enters your life has completed his or her assignment, that person moves on at no fault of yours or that person's. People move to other places, churches, cities or states. They may even move on to other relationships. It is alright. It is even healthy. Time is just up for the relationship that you shared. Mission accomplished. Knowing when a relationship is over is obvious, but accepting it is the difficult part. Chances are that you know when a friendship is over, but you keep hanging on when you know that there is nothing there. He or she doesn't call anymore. Shared interest has changed. They even missed your birthday. Let it go.

There is, however, a relationship that is designed to endure forever. It is between an Almighty Father and His humble children. We praise God for the lasting relationship He wants for His children. He desires to become intimate, (up close and personal), with us. His love has no boundaries. He will not leave us when times get bad. We can depend on Him to always be there for us. He is Jehovah Shammah: the God that is with us. What He does require is that we always place Him first. Our relationships with our friends, families and our things must be put in proper perspective. Nothing should be more important than God. "Take heed unto yourselves, lest ye forget the covenant of the Lord your God, which he made with you, and take you a graven image, or the likeness of any thing, which the Lord thy god hath forbidden thee; For the Lord thy God is a consuming fire, even a jealous God" (Deuteronomy 4:23 and 24). God will never forget your birthday. He will wake you up to celebrate right on time!

God desires to be a vital part of our lives. He is ready and willing to enter into our very situations at a moment's notice. "Behold, I stand at the door, and knock, if any man hears my voice and open the door, I will come in to him, and will sup with him, and he with me" (Revelation 3:20). God wants to commune/fellowship with us in a personal relationship. We hold the spiritual keys to our hearts. He permits us to make our own decisions of who we will allow to come in and who we will allow to stay. The door opens from the inside. When you hear His voice, harden not your heart. It is so sad that some hearts are weighed down with dead bolts and security locks, letting no love, no compassion nor mercy to enter.

FELLOWSHIP

God wants to fellowship with His children. One of the synonyms for the word fellowship in the *Reader's Digest Wordfinder* is 'participation.' In other words, where there is fellowship, there are two are more parties involved. No one can have fellowship alone. I cannot fellowship with you if you do not participate. God says that if you do not participate in this relationship that I (God) want to establish with you, then I cannot have fellowship with you! Notice that God said, "I am here. If you open the door, I will come in." You have to open the door and allow God's presence in your life. The word 'SUP' represents a spiritual communion between Christ and the faithful believer. God wants to fraternize with you. He wants to hang out with you. He wants a consistent relationship with you. He beckons you to come to him for fellowship, not just when there is a dire need, but God wants to be with you when all is well!

We allow people to come into our homes to socialize with us when

55

develop a closer association with them. We invite them to dinner, to parties or to small gatherings. We expect them to share as we share with them. God said if we would let Him in, He would 'sup' with us. He will share with us His goodness and His mercy. His goodness is inexhaustible and His mercy endures to all generations. The more we talk to Him and learn of Him, the less we sin against Him. When we enter into worship, prayer or praise, we become closer and closer to His greatness. He reveals truths that the world cannot understand. He opens up mysteries that geniuses cannot figure out. He gives us solutions to what seem to be impossible situations. He sups with us. He lets us enter into His Holy of Holies, to feel the joy of His salvation.

In this day of technology, we use electronic mail, FaceBook, Twitter, MySpace and the blog systems. Do we allow space for God in our lives or in our hearts? To add a person as a friend on FaceBook, permission is needed from the one being requested. God wants to be on our FaceBook friends' list. He wants to "twitter" with us. He wants to dialogue on our blogs. God is waiting on us to give Him permission to be on our MySpace. God is the most important guest that we will ever allow to come into our space!

The Israelites developed a warped relationship with the Egyptians, but managed to maintain a firm relationship with God. PROOF: In the wilderness many of them murmured and complained to Moses that it would have been better to die in Egypt than to die in the cold wilderness. "... I would rather be a doorkeeper in the house of my God, than to dwell in the tents of wickedness" (Psalm 84:10). Why go back to leeks and onions when God has promised a land flowing with milk and honey. Despite their murmuring and complaining, God blessed them with divine protection for 40 years. They were fed. Their clothes lasted. Healing took place when necessary. Jehovah Jireh was working in their lives. Sometimes we are so afraid of the unknown that we would rather suffer with the known. They knew what it was like in Egypt; they were sure of what they had and what they didn't have. They understood that it was a hard life in Egypt, but it was a life they had come to know. God was offering unchartered territory, a life that they did not know. Consequently, they were afraid. These behaviors exhibited a lack of faith. If God has delivered you into the marvelous light, accept it and trust Him to provide. At all cost, develop a relationship with Him that will cause you to trust Him.

Enoch walked with God, so much so that the Bible said he <u>was not</u>. Enoch released any will of his own to accept the will of God for his life. He experienced daily communion with God. His walk became so consecrated it was as though he was in GOD. Imagine levitating each day little by little. Each day, you are learning more and more about God and His goodness. The more you learn, the more you levitate. Each morning, God imparts more of His divine wisdom into your spirit and you are caused to levitate even more. Eventually you

-Relationships-

are so in God and He is so in you that you "are not." (*To be absent in the body is to be present with the Lord.*)

BOOSTERS

Everybody cannot fly in your orbit. When rocket ships are launched, along side of them are boosters. The boosters remain with the rocket until it is well into the flight journey. They eventually drop off. The rocket is now on its own to complete the mission. Some relationships are to act as boosters for us. They last long enough to get us boosted into what God has for us. He determines when they should enter into our lives and when they should leave. God knows who is needed and with what skill they have that will enhance our callings. I call them my "catalyst friends." They are around only for a jump start into my destiny. They present themselves right at the needed season. Just as God has the catalyst friends for us, sometime He uses us to be catalyst for others. Our responsibility becomes making sure that we are equipped for the job and not backing down from the challenge when presented.

Pastor Dorothy Norwood tells the story of praying for a lady in a church whose husband was practicing infidelity with a woman whose name was Sally. Pastor Norwood prayed for the woman.

The woman wanted her husband back home even though he did not work, did not pay any bills and did not treat her well. A time later, Pastor Norwood was again in a church service where this woman was present. Again, the lady returned to the prayer line with the same problem: her husband and Sally. She lived in close proximity to the other woman's house and the situation had not changed. He was still at her house and there was still a problem. Pastor Norwood exclaimed to her that she did not have the problem, Sally had the problem. Let him go!

The woman in the above story did not want to recognize what was actually going on in her life. She wanted to hold on to something she thought was good for someone else. God has made us whole in our own right. We do not have to be validated or approved of by anyone other than God. Often, Christ healed people of their sins and He concluded with "go your way because your faith has made you whole." Single Christians are whole. Divorced Christians are whole. In Christ Jesus, you are all that you should be and in Him; you have all that you need.

Developing a relationship with God is not accomplished over night. As in any human relationship, there will be times of doubt, insecurity, and bewilderment. It takes time and a sincere effort. We can grow as fast and as steady as we desire. God, in his infinite wisdom has very graciously provided us with a manual. It tells us of other God encounters and points to how we can have our own.

-Relationships-

When we look at people in the Word of God, we see ourselves. These biblical characters' lives serve as a mirror to us. We can identify with the mistakes made, the sins committed and the mercy needed and granted. David admitted his short comings and pleaded with God to give him a clean heart and renew the right spirit within him. This is our first step in developing a lasting relationship with God. We must admit that we fall short.

"I trust in God. He cares for me."

People Bondage: Free yourself and Let them go.

Chapter V

Loved Ones Who Have Passed On

Let it go...

One of the most difficult facets of life is the demise of someone who is most dear to us. The pain of a sudden death feels insufferable. The hurt associated with the loss of a child is unexplainable. Even the pain of loosing someone who has suffered for a lengthy period is difficult to withstand. I will not insult you by offering the statement, "Just get over it;" nor will I say, "Hold your head up high and don't cry." This is ludicrous. Death is stressful. Our bodies are built to release stress and crying is one of those mechanisms. When we are hurting, crying is a natural response. There are other avenues of expression, but we must carefully choose those that are not detrimental to us or to others. What we will do in this chapter is explore what the Bible says about death and give examples of how God wants us to handle it.

Many people will use the scripture that says "Let the dead bury the dead" as a means of helping the bereaved to move on with their lives. In Matthew 8 verses 18 through 22, Jesus is speaking to his disciples about loyalty and commitment - not neglect. He wants us to have priorities and structure in our lives. He is to always come first in our lives and in our decision making. "Trust in the Lord with all thine heart; and lean not unto thine own understanding. In all thy ways acknowledge Him and He shall direct thy paths" (Proverbs 3:5 & 6). It seems heartless to say to someone who has just lost a close loved one to let others take care of him or her and to just do as others say.

We must consider the fact that God knows all things. He knows the preparation needed to bury your loved one, if you are needed in the process and your particular state of being. Following God when all things are good and perfect is easy. What God wants you to realize is whether you are actually willing and obedient to follow Him when distressing situations occur or not. It is at these times that we must fully trust God. He wants us to be trustworthy and accountable regardless of our circumstances.

THE FAITH TEST

Sometimes, God gives us what I like to call 'faith tests'. These tests are unexpected quizzes that strengthen our faith and show us where we rank on the trust bar. The real test of our faith is measured by an actual experience rather than just our say so. My son, J, and his wife, Nicole, experienced a 'faith test' when they moved away from an established home with all their children, their furniture and their bills to another state. They trusted God to make the move because they felt that He had spoken to them to do so. They set out on a new adventure believing that they had heard a Word from God. They may have missed his precise directions because God had told them to go in one direction and they went another. God's course for our lives is usually explicit with no detours.

After a couple of months, their money began to run out. Neither of them had found work. Though it looked good and it was exciting, the first work experience (that was in the wrong city) did not work out because they were in the wrong place; they were out of order; they went in the wrong direction. When God says go right, you must go right. Always remember that God has a plan. They discovered that tuition and the car note were due. Diapers and gas were needed. There was enough stress to guide them to say, "Ok, let's try this again and go where we were instructed." Finally, they decided to follow God's plan and His direction.

In spite of everything, J and Nicole never lost hope. They never stopped seeking God. They never stopped believing God. They never stop praising Him. Throughout this whole ordeal, God always provided 'manna' from above. Everyday there were provisions. One Wednesday night they went to a church suggested to them by a friend. They introduced themselves as visitors from out of state who were settling into the city. In the introduction, J mentioned his profession. Now, J is a talented song writer, excellent musician, efficient director and anointed preacher (that was a mother describing her son). The pastor asked to speak with him after the service. There was a position in their music department available. Look at God! After a lengthy interview period and audition, J was offered the job of Minister of Music. Finally, someone had turned the light back on at the end of the tunnel. They were in the right city.

At last, a paycheck was forth coming! Remember, the enemy does not run out of monkey wrenches. He is prepared to chunk one your way at a moment's notice. J had been given the employee's hand book. In this book was a chapter that declared that the church required all of the new employees to practice the 'first seed' offering. This is an offering of the very first produce of your earnest harvest. It may be portions of your very first pay check or all of it. Please consider that my son had moved his family to a new city with limited funds. (And this was the second new city.) Again, he had a wife, a car note, and three children - one of which was in private school back home. He and his wife were animated about receiving that first check because they had not seen one in a very long time. The thought alone produced some financial comfort. They had purposed the money for tithes, bills, groceries and diapers, but the employee hand book required the first check to go back to the church.

My husband and I were visiting them and other family members in Houston when this occurred. My daughter-in-law initially came to me and asked, "Mom what would you do?" I sympathized for the dilemma that they were experiencing. My first thought was that you need to pay your tithes and your bills. The pastor will understand. The Holy Ghost was on his job arrested me and told me to tell them to pray; go to God about it. "In all thy ways acknowledge Him and He will direct your path" (Proverbs 3:6).

It was a Sunday Morning. J had to conduct two praise and worship services and had to make a decision regarding the check. Once we got to my sister's house for dinner, Nicole came to me and said that she and J had talked about what to do. They prayed together. They decided to turn the check in to the pastor. They made an appointment to see him after church. They remembered that God had taken care of them through every endeavor and He would continue to take care of them. "Casting all your care upon him; for *He careth for you" I Peter 5:7).*

All things work for the good! J and Nicole met with the pastor and were obedient to the Holy Spirit. They handed over the check to the pastor. He sat them down and explained to them that this was only a test of their faith and their obedience. The pastor needed to understand what level of faith they possessed. He handed the check back to J and told him to take care of his business. Nicole nearly fainted! Had he not walked in obedience this may not have worked in J's favor. It was a faith test. God knows what we are going through at all times. He is just seeing how we react in critical moments. Even when death occurs (death of our finances, spirits or a loved one), He still wants us to trust in Him. "Trust in the Lord with all thine heart; and lean not unto thine own understanding" (Proverbs 3:5).

Another crisis in our family was the death of my father. When my brother, sister and I met in Shreveport, Louisiana, to take care of the arrangements, we realized that Daddy had some money in the bank that would help defray some of the cost of the funeral. We needed that money. Off we went to the bank that Monday morning. The clerk informed us that because none of our names were on the checking account, we could not get any of the money. We told her that we did not want it for personal use; we just wanted her to write a check out to the funeral home to cover the cost. She said the law had recently changed and would not permit her to do that. Only our mother was allowed to withdraw any funds from my parents' account. We explained that our mother was in no condition to withdraw the money. In fact, she was in a nursing home in the early stages of dementia. She could not remember her name, least of all, write it. We were livid. We did not want any of the money to spend on ourselves. We wanted Daddy's money to bury Daddy! The bank representative refused. No amount of pleading or giving what we thought was a valid explanation worked. She followed the bank policy and we had to live with it!

Allow me a slight detour. In the early stages of my mother's dementia, she requested that I come to Shreveport, my home town, during a work week to sign papers that would allow me access to any of their funds. I was so discouraged at the thought of them not being there that I never returned home to take care of those critical matters. I was not ready to let go. It came back to haunt me. There was money to take care of things for my parents, but I failed to do what it took to receive access to it. Please let this be a lesson for all. If you have aging parents or any loved ones, it is crucial that you take care of money matters before it is too late. Have your name placed on bank accounts. Obtain power of attorney. Become executor of their estate. It is essential that you do whatever is necessary to gain access to funds upon death. Money can be tied up for years in legal mumbo jumbo! Consult a lawyer to see just what it is that you need to do.

As we left from the inside of the bank, it occurred to me what we had forgotten to do. My sister suggested that we go to my parent's lawyer to see what legal grounds we had. That was good and we did, but there was one vital thing that we failed to do. We did not pray. We made a circle in that very parking lot, acknowledged God and asked Him to direct our paths. We needed someone who would understand our plight. God hears and answers prayer. We went to the lawyer who indeed drafted a letter requesting the funds. We went to the nursing home and managed to get mama to sign the letter with what looked like a signature. Things seemed to be falling in place.

God directed us to another bank. It was across town, but that did not bother us. The person at this bank who was responsible for making that kind of decision was on her way to lunch. When the teller told her our need, she changed her plans. She brought us into her office and told us she would be glad to help us. She had recently lost her father and understood what we were facing. Look at God! Prayer is a set up. When you pray and do things God's way, blessings unfold. He will send you to whomever will be of assistance to you and He will fix their hearts to help you. We believe that God had already prepared the heart of this lady to help us. It was in her power to say yea or nay; but, it was God's power that answered our prayer. He supersedes the powers of man.

Isaiah 57:1 states, "The righteous perisheth, and no man layeth it to heart: and merciful men are taken away, none considering that the righteous is taken away from the evil to come." God knows what He is doing. If it was up to us, none of our loved ones would perish. We would choose everybody to go except the ones we love. Thank God that He makes these difficult, but important decisions of whom, when, where and how we leave this earth. His love is merciful. He will remove us from situations that He knows we cannot handle. That removal may be geographical, financial or even terminal: death. When it is geographical, it may be from one city to another.

When the removal is financial, it maybe from a lower income bracket to a higher one or vice-versa. God will do whatever He deems necessary to get us to trust Him. When the removal is by death, it may be so that suffering comes to a halt and the person is healed on the other side of death.

Our father was extremely hurt about what had happened to our mother. A few years prior to his death, my mother began to suffer with dementia. Daddy had shared a life with my mother for over 56 years and he could not fathom life without her. He took care of her as long as he could, but she needed care that he could not give. When her condition worsened and we were forced to place her in a nursing facility, he visited her often, but it was not the same. All of his children had moved out of town and he went home each day to an empty house. This house that had the sounds of people for many years was now empty and void of conversation, game playing, laughter and singing. All these things my father loved. After the children left, he still had Mama. Daddy longed for the early morning talks they had over a cup of coffee. He missed the warm feeling of her touch and her kisses. Even though her body was still present, the Leona he knew was gone; somewhere in her own little world. She was in a "Safe Place," but he could no longer reach her. He missed her.

My youngest sister, Patricia, assisted Daddy with most of his affairs. She would drive to Shreveport to help him with things he found puzzling. Unfortunately, she had the heartbreaking experience of witnessing his breaking down, crying and asking God why. Why did this have to happen to Leona, his sweetheart and partner for life? His heart just could not take it. When he died, my siblings found him on the floor. He may have grieved himself to death. He may have forgotten to take his medicine. He may have had a seizure and there was no one available to help as my mother would do. Whatever the cause, God knew. God took him home before he experienced another heart break. I trust God. Who knows, God may have saved him from the evil that was yet to come.

Paul puts it so gently for us in I Corinthians 5:8 and 9: "We are confident, I say, and willing rather to be absent from the body, and to be present with the Lord. Wherefore we labor, that whether present or absent, we may be accepted of him." We find comfort when our loved ones are gone when we have the security of knowing that they accepted Christ before departure. So when this earthly tabernacle has dissolved there is a place where we will be accepted by God. The exchange is from bodily casing to a spirit of immortality. The spirit will return to its Creator. How comforting it is to know that before 5 minutes are up, before the declaration of death by the coroner, before the hearse has taken the body, before the program is made and the announcement of death is made, the souls of the Saints are safely around the throne of God!

Grief: Thank God for the Memories and Let Them Go!

Chapter VI

RELIGION

Let it go...

What? You say let go of my religion? God forbid. With what reasoning is that? Please, allow me to explain. We used to sing a song when I was growing up in a Baptist Church choir that would ask, "Have you got good religion?"   After the song leader would ask the question, the choir would respond, "Certainly Lord!" "Have you got good religion? Certainly Lord! Have you got good religion? Certainly Lord; certainly, certainly, certainly Lord!" The choir would belt this out with mega force. The congregation would be up on their feet in jubilant praise with a 'yes Lord' on their lips answering the question with positive surety. I know I got good religion!

-Religion-

Although it was a religion that could be placed on the kitchen counter while I told you off, it was still a good religion. It also allowed me to stay home on rainy Sunday's to be sure that I would not get it wet; but it was a good religion. It was a religion of convenience; it could be pulled out like a trump card to deliver me when I was in trouble. Say what you will, it was a good religion. It was a good religion; certainly Lord!

What we have to take note of is the actual question: "Have you got good religion?" There are over 260 noted religions all over the world; religions that worship people, religions that worship the elements, religions that worship animals, religions that worship statues and religions that even worship myths. Religions have been formed and fashioned since the beginning of time. Statues of idol gods were made and reverenced in the Old Testament days. Shelves were carved into the walls of dwelling places to house these gods. Anybody could conjure up a religion to suit the needs. Psychologists warn us that all human beings need a higher power to believe. It is a part of our psyche to believe that there is something greater than we are governing the universe. We need something to accept as true whether it is good or bad. With this is mind, I issue the following warning: Be careful atheist; you may find yourself saying, "Oh Lord." No man is an island. We all need each other and we all need a god. The issue becomes choosing the right God.

In our quest to find a relatable creed, we experiment with whatever seems to work. We convince ourselves that this must be "the one" because it fits the situation or it is convenient because of the proximity to the home. Other rationales include: Services are held at times that fit a personal schedule; the concept is more compatible with what one chooses to believe; and on and on. Many religions start out with good intentions, but somewhere down the line, they may prove to be fallible. Some have stood the test of time and are secured with many followers, but there is only one that was in the beginning and will be here until the end. It is our duty to find the one true religion and accept its doctrine. Practicing a religion does not guarantee a good life here or in the hereafter. God instructed Joshua to tell the people in *Joshua 1:8, "This book of the law shall not depart out of thy mouth; but thou shalt meditate therein day and night, that thou mayest observe to do according to all that is written therein: for then thou shalt make thy way prosperous, and then thou shat have good success."* Good success only comes when we do it God's way. All other ground is sinking sand.

It is not a good religion that God is after when it comes to His people. The Pharisees were trying to establish a good and pure religion. They laid down laws that they did not keep themselves. They wanted rituals and doctrines to be enforced. Their target was those of the Jewish persuasion. They were constantly excluding all people who did not fit the mold. However, God has no respect of person. "*But glory, honor and peace, to every man that worketh good, to the Jew first, and also to the Gentile. For there is no respect of persons with God*" (Roman 2:9-11). What Jesus Christ did for us on the cross includes everyone who is willing to give up his or her will and to take on the will of God.

The suggestion then would be that we not concentrate on having a 'good religion,' but rather on having a good relationship with God. Our God is relational. Again, Saul is a good case in point. He is a primary example of having a religion, but not a relationship. He actually thought that he was helping God and the Roman government by persecuting Christians. He breathed out threats and slaughter against the disciples of the Lord. He went to the high priests to receive permission to bind Christians and to take them back to Jerusalem. Saul needed to learn a more excellent way. After a close encounter with Christ near Damascus, Saul changed his ways and God changed his name. Subsequently, Paul became an advocate for Christianity rather than a terrorist. He became, Paul, a chief Apostle of Jesus Christ. Paul let go of Saul and all he had been taught to pursue his Savior, Jesus Christ. "And straightway he preached Christ in the synagogues, that he is the Son of God" (Acts 9:19). If we would check ourselves, we might find some character flaws that we need to examine. We may possess some verbiage or ungodly actions that need to be speedily discarded. Perhaps an old personality needs to be changed or an ugly attitude softened or just maybe a tongue cleansed!

Enoch did not have religion. He had a relationship with God. For three hundred years, he walked with God. Enoch developed such a rapport with God that when it was time for him to depart this earth, the scripture says simply that "...he was not; for God took him" (Genesis 5:24). Again, can you imagine just levitating until you reach the Most High? He was not sick, not murdered, nor did he suffer an accident. Enoch just left with God. God has promised us in the book of Revelation that when Christ returns, we who remain shall be caught up to meet him in the air. We will be changed in a moment in the twinkling of an eye. Blessed are the ones who leave at the first resurrection. We will let the world go!

The question to answer now is this: How do I let go of religion and obtain a relationship with God? Several components come to mind, but none are difficult or impossible to accomplish. Foremost, there has got to be a yearning and hunger to know God. He is available to all of us. He wants to come and to sup with us. He stands at the door and knocks. "Behold, I stand at the door, and knock: if any man hear my voice, and open the door, I will come in to him, and will sup with him and he with me" (Revelation 3:20). This invitation was extended over 2,000 years ago and it has not expired. It was offered to the Jews first, to the Gentiles and to all who would accept Jesus the Christ as their personal savior. His work on the cross sealed the invitation. It allowed 'whosoever will' to come. To give us access to the Holy of Holies, the veil in the temple was rent from top to bottom.

Secondly, we must be consistent in our pursuit of God. It is easy to stop when our lives are busy with the cares of the world. An occasional prayer seems to suffice. Worship is for Sunday only. Praise is in to play only when something good happens to us. This is not good. There should always be room for God. "As the hart panteth after the water brooks, so panteth my soul after thee, O God" (Psalm 42:1).

BE SAVED

Before any relationship with God is formed, the person seeking the relationship must accept Him as his or her personal savior. "That if thou shalt confess with thy mouth the Lord Jesus and shalt believe in thine heart that God hath raised him from the dead, thou shalt be saved. For with the heart man believeth unto righteousness; and with the mouth confession is made unto salvation" (Romans 10:9-10.). This is the first step and it is an easy one. It is a two-part process: 1) Confess the Lord Jesus; and 2) believe in your heart that God has raised Him from the dead. There are no additives or supplements -only confess and believe. You don't have to be so, so saved; just saved. Just believe and confess. No blood has to be shed nor animal sacrifice made. It has already been done on a cross at Calvary. You have been given full access to the Kingdom of God and His everlasting salvation.

Salvation is not temporary; it is permanent. You cannot pick it up and put it down. It must be perpetual in your spiritual growth. Salvation is a way of life. There is no gray area. You are either saved or you're not. You either believe or you don't. You did not choose salvation; God chose it for you. Salvation is a gift from God. You cannot earn it or buy it; just accept it. It is a gift. "For by grace are ye saved through faith; and that not of yourselves: it is the gift of God" (Ephesians 2:8). However, you can be saved, having received the gift, and be unaware of the benefits. When you do not accept the entire Bible as truth, you live beneath the privileges of salvation. Believe the Word for all that it says you can have, what it says you can be and who it says you are.

When interviewing for a job, the first question asked may be, "Are you qualified?" The second question is usually, "What is the salary?" The probability of promotion should be explained. Work hours are discussed. Dress is considered. How often and what day is pay day is also a topic of discussion. Yet somewhere in the interview, the question will be, "Are there any fringe benefits?" In other words, I know you are going to pay me what the job is worth, but are there any extras – any supplements to the wages? What does it take to be promoted? How soon can I go on vacation? How are the sick hours accumulated? Are there any personal days, 401k or retirement plans? Just what are the benefits?

The word fringe means border. It is that which hangs at the bottom of the garment. Even though it may be attached to the garment, it is considered dispensable - not totally necessary. It could be left off. In the Old Testament, a blue fringe was placed at the border of the priest's garment. It was not the robe, but it was placed on the hem of the garment to remind the people of the covenant God had made. Every time they would see that border they knew that God was going to bless them. They were reminded of the promises of God and His covenant with them. Because God is not a man that He should lie, the people were assured and confident in the very thought of reaching the Promised Land.

Benefits are considered the advantage, subsidy or the profit. Thus, fringe benefit has a monetary value, but it does not affect the basic wage. Some jobs come with fringe benefits that actually outweigh the wages. If the job offers insurance, stock options, 401k, etc., it is well worth considering. Never leave an interview without discussing the fringe benefits. You may find out the job may pay less, but offers a quicker way up the corporate latter with significant remuneration along the way. In comparison, our Christian journey may seem difficult at best, but when you think of the outcome, it makes you want to endure until the end! Going up the rough side of the mountain is easier to climb than the smooth side where you can keep sliding downward.

State Farm had a commercial that explained a policy that offered a check to any of its policy holders who were accident free for 6 months. That's a fringe benefit. Similarly, if at the end of the year store sales have remarkably increased, the employees may get a bonus check. This is a fringe benefit. A matriarch in the lineage of Jesus, Ruth gleaned the reaping from the harvest after working in Boaz's filed. She was able to take home the perks that she gathered from the job. This was a fringe benefit.

Another exemplar, Solomon was a King for God. When asked what he desired from God, he replied, "... an understanding heart to judge thy people." These words pleased God. God said, "Because you did not ask for yourself long life, or riches, or the life of your enemies. I have done according to thy words." Then God added the fringe benefit, "And I have also given thee that which thou hast not asked, both riches, and honor: so that there shall not be any among the kings like unto thee all thy days" (I Kings 3:13). These were fringe benefits. Because of Solomon's integrity and selflessness, he was awarded fringe benefits before the job began.

With God, the ultimate payday is when we see Him face to face. Lyrics to an old song said, "Just one moment in God's Kingdom will pay for it all." This is our Christian goal: to see Jesus. But my dear brothers and sisters, we can enjoy some fringe benefits along the way.

RECEIVE THE BAPTISM OF THE HOLY GHOST

Paul asked the disciples of Ephesus if they had received the Holy Ghost. Their answer was that they did not even know of the Holy Ghost. "He said unto them, have ye received the Holy Ghost since ye believed? And they said unto him, we have not so much as heard whether there be any Holy Ghost" (Acts 19:2). Paul began to preach to them and "...laid hands upon them, the Holy Ghost came on them; and they spake with tongues and prophesied." This scripture alone lets us know that there are some who believe, but do not possess the Holy Ghost. New converts must be taught the Word of God and be introduced to the benefits and privileges of being saved.

For many years, I believed confessing belief in Christ produced all that was available to me. I believed that upon confession I received the Holy Ghost and that it was His job to make me live right. What I did not know was that there was more. I was saved, but there was more. I was introduced to the meaning of *John 7:38 and 39: "He that believeth on me, as the Scripture hath said, out of* his belly shall flow rivers of living water. But this spake He of the Spirit, which they that believe on Him **should receive**..."

Living without the Holy Ghost is like receiving a house fully furnished as a gift but using only one room. Pretend that you are given a luxurious house as a gift. The house is thoroughly furnished. You have the keys. There are five bedrooms with adjacent bathrooms, a large kitchen, family room, dining and living rooms. You choose to dwell in just the family room, but you have access to the entire house. Admittance is given to all parts of the house, but you remain in that one room. This is living beneath your privileges.

You must be baptized in the Holy Ghost. Welcome Him into your heart and into your life, then you will have a personal encounter with God. The Holy Ghost, the *parakletos*, is the One who walks along side of you. He is present for you as a comforter and a guide. Let go of your foolish pride and antiquated beliefs. God has promised not to leave you comfortless or without direction. He has sent the Holy Ghost for your good. If you have not shared this experience, talk with your pastor or an elder of the church to pray with you and to show you what God says about receiving the baptism of the Holy Ghost.

STUDY GOD'S WORD

II Timothy 2:15. "Study to show thyself approved unto God, a workman that needeth not to be ashamed, rightly dividing the word of truth." Studying the Word of God is essential to our Christian walk. God opens doors that no man can close and closes doors that no man can open through His Word as we daily walk with Him. This is where we learn about God. It is impossible to form a relationship with someone you don't know. The Bible is an inspired autobiography of God. It tells us all about Him and His love for creation. From Genesis to Revelation, the love of God is expressed.

Benjamin Franklin once said, "An investment in knowledge always pays the best interest." Though it was for secular purposes, it is certainly applicable for spiritual well being. Our spiritual connection with God is an investment for our souls. The Bible is our contract and we must know what is in our contract that it may be beneficial to us. We don't know our rights until we read and learn the contract. A good example is when your refrigerator breaks down and you fall apart. Only negative thoughts arise, "I bet it's the compressor, it's an unknown part that is not manufactured any more or something expensive." You haven't read the Warranty, so you don't know that you actually have one more month of free maintenance and parts because you haven't read the contract. The contract guarantees your insurance!

With any contract, there is fine print. There are mysteries in the Bible that I can't explain. The Holy Spirit is present to decipher those parts of the contract that I need, but don't quite understand. I have learned that I don't need to know everything, but what I do need to know, God reveals unto me if I open up to Him. Some good information I receive from God is revealed on a *Need-To-Know Basis.* Right now, I know everything that I need to know for this exact moment, therefore, the enemy can not beat me up with what I don't know. When the opportunity presents itself for me to learn, I must seize the moment! When I learn all that I can about God, the better I am - the more ammunition I have to fight the devil. When I continue to seek to know my God, the more spiritual I am, the more humble I am and the less I sin against Him!

We study the Word of God because it progressively unfolds the Truth. Man has always searched for the truth. Even in the Garden of Eden, Eve desired the truth. The Word of God is TRUTH. The Old Testament is the New Testament concealed and the New Testament is the Old Testament revealed. The Word of God is both *Logos* and *Rhema.* Logos is the thoughts that were in the heart of God before the creation, an efficient power that changes the life of man from sinner to saint. This is the desired effect. Rhema is that which is spoken - that which is uttered in speech or writing. It is the word that the believer receives from the Spirit. Rhema is what we study, what we grow by and what guides us through life.

DEVELOP A STRONG PRAYER LIFE

It is good to have an established prayer life. When you go to the same bank for all of your transactions, the teller will not only learn your name, but sometimes she will remember your account number because she is familiar with you. It becomes easier to have a check cashed when the teller knows who you are. In a greater way, God needs to be familiar with you. He needs to know you. You should cry out to Him so much that He knows your particular cry. As mothers, we know a hunger cry from an 'I'm wet cry.' We know an 'I'm hurt cry' from an 'I just need attention cry.' It is because we have that relationship with our children that we understand each cry. In a like manner, when you have developed a personal relationship with God, He knows and understands every cry you make. That relationship is formed when you pray in season and out of season, when you are sick and when you are well, when you feel the pains of hunger and when you are full. God knows and answers prayer!

Build momentum with your prayers. Momentum serves as an invisible force that propels you. When riding a bicycle at a fast rate of speed, at some point you can stop peddling so vigorously and just glide. You have built up momentum. When you are in daily prayer with the Father, when the enemy catches you off guard, when timing is critical and there is no quiet place to go, with an established momentum you are able to ask God to use one of those prayers that you have already sent up!

When I was a little girl, there was an area behind our neighborhood we dubbed 'Motor Cycle Hill.' It was a wooded area full of pine straws, hills and danger, but it was great for bicycle riding. Our parents were reluctant to give us permission to play there because of the adult motorcyclist activity. Apparently, it was good for motorcycle riding as well as for bicycle riding. My friends and I just wanted to ride our bikes. We were children, so we went anyway. At the entrance, there was a very deep 'V' shaped incline. To get over into the area where we could ride, we would have to build up enough speed and momentum going down the incline that when you reached the bottom you could actually skip over the valley and jump to the other side going up. If you did not have enough speed to do this, you would slide back down and get stuck at the bottom. You would need assistance to get out of the valley. If you went alone, you had to be sure that you were proficient enough to make the jump. On the other side was the joy of free cycle riding, you know, wind blowing on our faces and through our hair.

If we have built up momentum in our prayer lives, when trouble comes, our previous prayers will act as catalysts for us. When it looks like we are on an incline, our prayers are there to pull us through, causing us to skip the valley and to go right up to the top to reach our promised land. There is not always the opportunity to go through a ritual of prayer. Sometimes we don't know what to say, but if we have prayed, God knows our voices and He hears our cries. God is faithful to rescue us. He is a present help in the time of trouble!

I submit to you that it is your God given right to pray. You and I have a right to pray. When there is a need, I pray. When there is not a need, I pray. When I am in trouble, I pray. When I'm not in trouble, I pray. I choose to pray rather than to worry. I build momentum with my prayers. I cannot worry and pray and I cannot pray and worry!

Unfruitful Religion: Let it go

Chapter VII

DIABETES: WHO ME?

Let it go.....................

To find out that you may have an interminable disorder can be disturbing. The news can take you for such a surprise that it is very difficult to digest. Denial is the response for about the first 12 months and if there is no visible change, it may last even longer. When I was diagnosed with diabetes, my first response was, "Who me? Couldn't be!" I am not a bread eater nor do I consume enormous amounts of sugar infested foods. A little ice cream every now and then satisfies my sweet cravings. Since turning 50, I have tried to be somewhat careful regarding my intake of food. I have tried to live my daughter's concept: moderation is the key. I very seldom over indulged in even my most favorite treats, so I thought.

Being spiritually profound, heredity (family medical history) should not apply to me. No, not me! What has affected family members in the past is just that: them and the past. Why me? Why was I given this news? Don't I get credit for my attempt at a healthy lifestyle? Am I not above the average? Never mind that I have family members in my immediate family living with these conditions, but we are not talking about them we are talking about me. That's them; this is me the one who plays the game as instructed. This just should not be. I don't want this. I can't use diabetes. It does not enhance my life one iota. I have done everything that I am supposed to do. I even exercise ever so often!

I believe strongly in the truth which limits my accepting facts. The world offers facts - the Word offers truth. You understand the fact from the doctor's report is that you are sick, but the truth says by His stripes you are healed (Isaiah 53:5). You know the fact says you are broke, but the truth says He shall supply all of your needs according to His riches in glory by Christ Jesus (Philippians 4:19). That was and still is what I preach. Then why is it that my blood sugar numbers are so high? Maybe the test was faulty. Maybe it is just temporary. We will check in a few months to see if we get the same results. Surely, this could not be happening to me. Do I accept the facts or the truth?

I tried to pray it away. I made daily confessions against it. I would not allow the word diabetes to come out of my mouth. Whenever people would ask did I have diabetes, I would say, "No, that's what someone else said or that's what they say." Never would I admit that there was something physically and possibly permanently wrong with me. It worked! I improved for a short while and even took myself off of my medication because I was healed. I maintained my confession that I was healed. I started a more stringent exercise regime. I started drinking diet drinks and I even measured what I was eating. I cut down on the rice, potatoes and sandwiches. I drank more water. Guess what? The numbers were good for a little while, but when old eating habits gradually returned, so did the negative meter readings.

Acceptance of something that you don't want is a hard pill to swallow. I could not let go of the evil eating habits. Even though I would not let go of my confession, I still wanted to eat whatever I desired. I like German chocolate cake, ice cream and Oreo cookies. This did not work. My lifestyle and mind set had to be enduringly changed. One friend of mine told me, "You have had a year of denial; it is time to get over it and face facts." This is probably good advice for some, but it was not for me. My stand is *I will do what I have to do until my body lines up with my confession.* My confession is that I am healed, but along with the confession comes faith and work. Faith without works is dead! Healing comes with responsibility. I realized that I have to believe God and work on my bad habits. It is up to me to take charge of my condition instead of allowing my condition to take charge of me.

Consider what I said and what I did. In this scenario what I had to let go of was old habits. This has to be permanent, not for just a moment. Old bad habits must be permanently put to an end. As long as I was doing what was right for my body I maintained good healthy blood pressure, glucose and cholesterol numbers; but as soon as I faltered, things changed and I stepped back into the danger zone. Romans 12:2: "Be not conformed to this world, but be ye transformed by the renewing of your mind." I had to make a concerted effort in my mind to change. I had to renew my mind.

The first step was taking responsibility of the damage. I had to release the denial, admit the fact that was presented to me and then act on it by doing what was required by natural law. Our doing what is right will cause the TRUTH to manifest. Now, God requires that we trust Him, but He also requires that we do that which is right. Your body is the temple of God and you are held liable for taking care of it. "Know ye not that ye are the temple of God, and that the Spirit of God dwelleth in you (I Corinthians 3:16)?"

I confronted my nurse practitioner, as though it was her fault, with my not understanding why I was diagnosed with diabetes. I needed to know what exactly had I done wrong. This did not show up until the children were out of the house,most large bills paid and life was about to begin again. She explained to me that there was a little gene that I had at birth. I did nothing to cause it, nor anything to feed it. It was just a part of my makeup.

Her explanation reminded me of Job. Job was perfect and an upright man who feared God and eschewed evil. After tremendous lost of family and belongings, Job was afflicted with boils from the sole of his feet to the crown of his head. His wife suggested that he curse God and die. His friends suggested that all his troubles were a result of his sins (Job chapters 1 and 2). They did not come for moral support, but rather to criticize and show how upright they were. **SIDEBAR: WHENEVER PEOPLE HAVE TO CONSTANTLY TELL YOU WHO THEY ARE IN CHRIST AND SHOW UP YOUR FLAWS, THEY ARE SUFFERING FROM SERIOUS INSECURITIES.** Job had to let them go. Job chose to continue to trust God. He fell on his knees and worshiped God. In the end Job received double for his trouble.

When you find out your body's disposition not to tolerate certain foods, then you should avoid them or at least treat them as an enemy. (You will tease your enemy for just so long and then he will get serious and stop playing with you and the consequences maybe detrimental.) Remember, you are the temple that God has to use. If the temple is dilapidated and run down, its production will be slow or void. Christ cursed the fig tree because it was not producing and it withered away (Matthew 21:19). The leaves were there, but there was no fruit. It was useless. God expects us to produce fruit in our season. The fig tree was not only unfruitful, but it did not have what was necessary to produce. There was no taqsh*. Taqsh is a little bud on the back of the leaf that produces the fruit. We must be careful not to eat those things that would cause us not to grow our tasqh (*"*Hard Sayings of the Bible*"; Kaiser, Davids, Bruce, Brauch, 1996)!

Living in denial is not a way of God. He wants you to be a good steward over your health, your finances and your soul. "Beloved, I wish above all things that thou mayest prosper and be in health, even as thy soul prospereth" (John 3:1:2). Salvation is a 'whole' concept. It is not a partial notion. God does not want you to be rich and sick, smart and crazy nor saved and foolish. He wants you whole. When He healed Jarius' daughter he said to her, "Daughter, be of good comfort: thy faith hath made thee whole, go in peace" (LUKE 8:48). Jesus asked the man at Bethesda, "Wilt thou be made whole?" (John 5:6). Responsibility comes with being healed and made whole. Christ was asking if he would be accountable if healed and made whole. This means letting excuses for yourself and denial of your condition go. It means standing up and saying, "It is what it is, but God is still in charge."

We have to let go of denial. Face facts and apply the truth. We need to live responsibly and maturely, knowing that there is nothing that God cannot change. There is no disease too hard for God. Nothing with Him is impossible. Natural laws of nature and health must be respected. Don't eat three pork shops and a plate of ribs if you know you have high blood pressure. Leave the cake for skinny Sally who is 5'11" and 120 pounds. Take your prescribed medicines and exercise. God has given the doctors knowledge to help us stay here longer. Be obedient to those who know better than you. God will honor your faithfulness and good sense. He will allow your body to line up with your confession if you take responsibility of your health. Live responsibly.

Certain issues in our lives build our character. They help us to see what another person has to handle who has similar issues. I see people on dialysis or who have lost their sight or have a limb amputated, and my attitude toward them has changed. Just as our life dispositions are different so are the tracks we run. Your track may be the outer lane with bumps and scrapes that you feel are innumerable. I may have the inner lane, which you think is shorter and easier, but may have bigger bumps and cause larger scrapes. Somehow, I had begun to think that I was indispensable; indestructible. Little did I know that God had a plan for my life that would cause me to live with more compassion and cause me to depend on Him even more than I had before. Now, understand the Lane may be positioned differently, but it is the same track. It may take different maneuvering, but it is the same track. We may not finish at the same time, but is the same track. It is called life. God giveth and God taketh away. Blessed be the Name of the Lord!

We must continue to pray for healing while knowing that God's grace is sufficient. If he decides to allow a disease to progress or remain as is, it is well. If he chooses to heal on this side of heaven or on the other side of heaven, it is well. We must trust God. He knows what it takes to make us into the men and women that we should be. His thoughts toward us are of peace and not evil to get us to an expected end! Our job is to take responsibility of our temples. It is as important as reading the Bible.

Satan confronted God about his servant Job. He wanted the hedges removed from Job's life. Satan felt that Job would curse God if he didn't have it so easy. God granted him the wish, but he told him not to mess with Job's soul. Notice, before satan could do anything to Job, he had to get permission from God. I no longer live in denial. Everything that gets to me must go by God first. Does facing the FACTS change my belief in the TRUTH, not at all? I believe God. I trust His will for my life and I continue to confess the TRUTH!

Denial: Let it go.

Chapter VIII

POSSESSIONS

Let them go.......

Possessions are things. What do we do with things? We turn them into idols. Ever notice how quickly a new car is scratched, nicked or damaged? We do all that we can to protect it. We park miles away from other cars in a parking lot whether it is crowded or not. We may even park across the division lines to keep another vehicle from getting too close. Our 'things' are important to us. We praise them and put them on pedestals. We hold on to them because we believe them to be prized collectables. We dust or wash them and place them on a shelf. Then two weeks later, we dust them or wash them and place them back on the shelf. We repeat this scenario until the things get so old that we don't care about them anymore, but we will never throw them away.

-Possessions-

Things accumulate. Clothes that we have not worn in 10 years remain in our closets because when we look at them (knowing it was 100 pounds ago when we last wore them) and say I might still wear that if I loose a pound or two. We even have utensils in our kitchens that we haven't used nor looked at in the last 5 years. We keep old magazines because we might just want to read that article again or there may be one I missed reading. We will drive an old car until it completely falls apart at the point that it has to be replaced and then we keep the old one in the back yard. Why? We replace items, but we don't throw the old items away. Someone should write a book about letting things go. Oh, yeah, I did!

Spiritually speaking, we belong to God. He created us in His own image. He, and only He, has the authority and the power to govern our lives. Colossians speaks of his preeminence. "For by Him were all things created, that are in heaven and that are in earth, visible and invisible, whether they be thrones, or dominions, or principalities, or powers: all things were created by Him, and for Him. And He is before all things, and by Him all things consist..." (Colossians 1:16 and 17). In other words, God is above all things and in Him all things consist. That Greek word consist means 'held together' (Key Word Study Bible Lexical Aid to the New Testament). Thus, 'in Him all things consist' simply means that Christ holds all things together. He holds our finances together. He holds and keeps our marriages together. He holds our emotions together.

The enemy desires to sift us as wheat, but thank God, He holds us together!

There is no one greater, no one more powerful and yet more merciful than God! What an awesome God we serve. The same One who gives us life and has the power to take it, is the same One who grants us mercy and extends life. We are His children and He is our Father. He watches over us to protect and guide us in any situation that may occur in our lives. Our duty is to take everything to God in prayer! Nothing should supersede our relationship with God. There is no possession worthy of placement before Him!

We are God's possession. The earth is the Lord's and the fullness thereof, the world and they that dwell therein. The things that we acquire don't really belong to us. Sure, we paid or we are still paying on the dream house, but the wood, the brick and mortar belong to God. All things belong to the Creator. He just allows us to use them. We breathe His air. We drink His water. We eat his vegetables and live stock. It all belongs to God. So why do we have such a difficult time giving away that which is not ours to hoard in the first place?

The rich young ruler approached Jesus wanting to know what good thing could be done so that he would earn eternal life. He felt that he had kept all the commandments and he needed to know if there was something else necessary to be saved. Jesus told him to "...go and sell that thou hast, and give to the poor, and thou shalt have treasure in heaven: and come and follow me. But when the young man heard that saying, he went away sorrowful: for he had great possessions" (Matthew 19:16-22). Nothing we own should be indispensable to us. If tragedy strikes, you would learn how to make it in life without some of the luxuries you presently enjoy. The rich man felt that he had accumulated numerous possessions and they were too precious and special to him to give away. It was too hard and took too long to attain such wealth and he just could not see parting with his treasures. After all he had led a good wholesome life. He kept the commandments. What more could be required of him? He felt that he deserved his earning. He had possessions that he could not let go!

We must examine ourselves to see what it is that we have (material things) that we cannot let go. What is so important to us that we can't live without? Things are not invincible, but they are replaceable. Suppose we were in Job's position whose substance was lost in a day's time. "And there came a messenger unto Job, and said, "The oxen were plowing, and asses feeding beside them: And the Sabeans fell upon them and took them away; yea they have slain the servants with the edge of the sword and I only am escaped alone to tell thee." While he was yet speaking there came another: the sheep are burned up and the servants consumed and I only am escaped along to tell thee. While he was yet speaking there came another: the Chaldeans fell upon the camels and have carried them away. While he was yet speaking there came another: thy sons and thy daughters were eating and drinking wine and there came a great wind and smote them. All of the young men are dead" (Job 1:14-19).

Finally, Job shows us how we are to react to tragedy in Chapter 1, verse 20: "Then Job arose, and rent his mantle and shaved his head, and fell down upon the ground and worshipped." Job never cursed God or charged Him for his problems. He maintained a spirit of worship. God is always looking at how we react to precarious situations. We can display an attitude of trust or one of distrust. Trusting God will show up in our temperance (restraint or control) and meekness (strength under control). If we can maintain an air of meekness in the midst of loosing then temperance is our virtue. Can we loose and still worship God? At the end, we know that God blessed the latter end of Job more than his beginning. We must love and trust God more than we do our things. He knows His thoughts toward us and they are thoughts of peace and not evil to get us to an expected end.

God blesses us with things when He knows He can trust us. My good friend, Harry Moore, used to say, "If I cannot handle $20, God will give me $19.99 until I can handle the other penny." We must be faithful over a few things before he will make us ruler over many things. Christ's parable of the talents in Matthew 25:23-29, gives us the perfect example. It tells the story of the lord who delivered unto his servants his goods. To one he gave 5 talents, to another 2 talents and to another 1 talent. He gave to each man according to his ability. This lord proceeded to go on a long journey. The one who received the 5 talents went and traded with the same and made 5 more talents. The one with two talents gained 2 more talents, but the one with only 1 talent hid the talent by burying it in the earth.

When the lord returned, he found the servant that had been issued 5 talents and the servant who was given 2 talents both multiplied what that had been given. They gained interest. The lord declared to them, "...Well done, good and faithful servant; thou has been faithful over a few things, I will make thee ruler over many things: enter thou into the joy of thy lord." Finally, the one who was given the 1 talent came forth. His excuse for not causing his talent to increase was, "Lord, I knew thee that thou art a hard man, reaping whether thou hast not sown and gathering where thou has not strewed. And I was afraid and went and hid thy talent in the earth: lo, there thou hast that is thine" (Matthew 25:24b-25). His lord's answer was, "Thou wicked and slothful servant, thou knewest that I reap where I sowed not, and gather where I have not strewed, thou oughtest therefore to have put my money to the exchangers, and then at my coming I should have received mine own with usury. Take therefore the talent from him and give it unto him which hath ten talents" (Matthew 25:26-28).

Matthew 25:29 is the conclusion of the matter. "For unto every one that hath shall be given, and he shall have abundance: but from him that hath not shall be taken away even that which he hath." When God instructs us to 'occupy' until he comes, he is encouraging us to make full proof of the abilities that he has given us. Our talents are for purpose. Proverbs 18:16 says, "A man's gift maketh room for him, and bringeth him before great men." Use what you got! Market your gifts. If you have the gift of gab, study to become a lawyer. If you have keen foresight, make politics your interest. If you are good with your hands and can cut a piece of wood without cutting off your finger, see if carpentry would be profitable for you. If you are a singer, or dancer, or speaker, look into fields that would cause you to use your talent. Never sit on your talents. Develop them and let them go to work for you!

AN EMOTIONAL CLEAN-UP

There is a popular television show on cable titled *Clean House.* During the one hour of the show, cleaning experts come in and view homes that are rather disorderly. They size up the job, (to determine how much money is needed), have a yard sale, match the proceeds up to one thousand dollars and commence to changing a mess into a small mansion. Each worker has a particular area of expertise. There is an efficient organizer, a go to man who actually fixes old furniture and a designer for the decor. The cleaning team's job is to convince the homeowner to divest the home of some old things that are not necessary in their lives and put them in a yard sale. The family has to decide what goes and what stays. The "rule of thumb" is that if you have not used it in six months or worn it in a year, you should get rid of it.

Before the actual discarding of unused items, the host sits with the homeowner to get to the root of the problem. They discuss the underlying reason for holding on to stuff that has not been used in a very long time. Emotions are flared. Old hurts are brought to the surface, all in an attempt to release emotional stains of the past. The homeowners have to reach inside of themselves and figure out what is the real problem. The question has to be answered, "Why have I become a hoarder?" Often times we don't want to rid ourselves of emotional baggage simply because we have repressed the problem and we do not want to face the past and the reasons why.

The removal of unused items is crucial, but changing a lifestyle starts in the mind. Hoarders are of the mindset that whatever they see, they need. They buy things that they already possess. These things may be on sale or at a good price that the hoarder feels they just can't pass up. The need is not there, but the greed is present. They will continue to buy, obtaining things until the spending is completely out of control. Hoarders have homes that are unlivable. They will tell you that they just can't stop buying no matter how hard they try. Until the mind is changed everything remains the same. The leader of *Clean House* will always have a talk with the homeowners about changing their present life style. She knows that if the mind isn't changed, things will go back to the way they were before all of the hard work is done to clean the hoarders' home. The homeowners must release a mind to hoard and gain a mind to let things go!

Possessions: Let them go!

Chapter IX

PRIDE

Let it go.......

God's timing is impeccable. He allows us to be in the right place at the right time; even when we are not aware. Several years ago I had the blessed opportunity of speaking at a Christian Women's retreat in Houston, Texas. The room was set up with two sets of pews separated by an isle down the middle. During the conference there was a session of prayer where we were told to pair up with someone from across the room - preferably with someone we did not know. I was actually looking for my friend, Minister Tarsha Jackson because I knew her to be a strong Woman of God who could get a prayer through, but I had to be obedient and find someone I did not know. That was easy because I was not from Houston and most of the people there I did not know. My prayer partner and I hooked up immediately without ever having laid eyes on each other before the conference. It was a divine connection. I was prepared to take the lesser role, but I felt a sense of urgency in her spirit. I sensed fear, maybe stemmed from an unknown source. Therefore, I knew that I was to take the lead so I began to pray. We prayed and then we talked.

She felt comfortable with me so she began to share some personal issues. She let me know of some of the things that were going on in her life, one of which was a health issue. I tried to encourage her with what I knew God could do. We talked about Isaiah 53:5: "But he was wounded for our transgressions, he was bruised for our iniquities: the chastisement of our peace was upon him, and with his stripes we are healed." I explained to her that the word **HEALED** had an 'ed' on the end of it which indicated past tense. She is already healed in the Spirit. Our job is to believe the confession we make with our mouths and to wait on our bodies to line up with our confessions. I also reminded her that God is Jehovah Rapha - the God who heals, and that there is nothing too hard or any disease too devastating for Him. I further encouraged her to never stop believing God no matter what the situation or circumstances look like. She received my words with gratitude and we both vowed to stay in touch with praise reports. We thanked God for healing and the new relationship.

The following Sunday, I attended the church who sponsored the conference. After the services were over, my brother was standing outside of the church with me greeting people as we waited on other family members to come out of the sanctuary. The lady I had prayed for approached me to introduce me to her husband. After she introduced us, she said to her husband with tears in her eyes, "This is the woman who changed my life." I simply hugged her, said a "God Bless you" and shook hands with her husband. What she said was sweet, but nothing more. Nothing registered with me but the fact that she was grateful for what God was about to do in her life and with her health. Even though she felt that I was greatly instrumental in the change in her life, I knew that I was just the messenger of good news. It was my pleasure!

When she and her husband departed, my brother looked at me and asked me, "How does that feel?" I said, "How does what feel?" He said, "How does it feel to know that you have changed someone's life. That must be an incredible feeling to know that you have made such an impact by what you said." My response to him was, "I don't know how it feels. I've never thought about it." If it were me making the change, I guess I would be overjoyed with pride; but I'm intelligent enough to know that it is not me. A change in life comes when the person involved makes a decision to let go and to let God. I was just an instrument used to get her to understand where and who she was in God. I get to witness, but God gets the Glory.

-Pride-

Being oblivious to what is taking place keeps one with an attitude of humility.   If God would allow us to relish in every blessed event when someone is healed or even encouraged by what we say in His stead, we would get besides ourselves as some have done!   The healing comes from God. The ability to speak and to know what to say comes from God. The gift to comfort comes from God. The anointing to pray and to lay hands comes from God. Knowing who He is and His power keeps me grounded. You can only continue to work for God if you remain grounded. It is not about me, it is about God! "And said, If thou wilt diligently hearken to the voice of the Lord thy God, and wilt do that which is right in his sight, and wilt give ear to his commandments, and keep all his statues, I will put none of these diseases upon thee, which I have brought upon the Egyptians: for I am the Lord that healeth thee" (Exodus 15:26).

Misplaced glory is fuel and ammunition for the enemy. When God uses us, for whatever purpose, we must constantly remind ourselves that it is His doing not our own, no matter how marvelous in our sight. There are some of us who thrive on compliments and ego stroking. It is normal. It is only when we take it to the extreme, do we lose touch of where our gifts and talents originate. The enemy loves it. He knows that vanity is a human weakness. If he can catch us in a vulnerable moment, he can feed our ego enough to make us believe our abilities are within ourselves rather than in the One who is the source of our accomplishments. It is He who has made us and not we ourselves. Be thankful unto Him and bless His name.

Proverbs 16:18: "Pride goeth before destruction and haughty spirit before a fall." A quick way to a fall is to attempt to take the glory of God as your own. When you begin to believe that what you do is done because of who you are and not because of whom God is, a fall is imminent. Never mind singing, "If I am too high Lord, bring me down." He will. He will not share His glory with man. "I am the Lord: that is my name: and my glory will I not give to another, neither my praise to graven images" (Isaiah 42:8). To everything give Him thanks for this is the will of God concerning you; not my will but thy will be done.

When someone blesses you with a compliment, a simple "Thank You" is always in order. Over kill such as these ruins the compliment: "Oh I just praise God. The glory belongs to God. What I do is for Him only. I'm just blessed by God. Praise Him." Just say thank you, walk away and quietly give God praise and tell Him thank you. My husband and I have three talented, gifted children. Our middle son is a preacher, musician and songwriter. He has done numerous music workshops. Some time ago when he was still living with us, I passed by his room. He was on the phone. Apparently someone was giving him praise for something he had done. All I could hear him say was, "Praise God, The Glory belongs to God. God is so good." I stopped and said, "Just tell the woman thank you. You are entering into overkill!" Anointed people never have to convince other people of how humble they are. If it is sincere, they will see it. "Thank you" is polite and sufficient. God knows our heart regardless of what our lips are saying.

IT'S A HEART ISSUE

In II Chronicles 26, there is the story of Uzziah who was made king at only 16 years of age. He reigned 52 years in Jerusalem. Uzziah was a very prominent king. He was a relative of Isaiah and a great influence in the king's life. Uzziah was an extremely smart man with quite a few accomplishments. In the beginning, he did that which was right in the sight of the Lord. As long as he sought the Lord, God made him to prosper. He built up cities and tore down enemy walls. Uzziah fortified armies. He won battles against the Philistines and the Arabians. In Jerusalem, he made engines (weapons) to shoot arrows and great stones in war.

Verse 16 says, "But when he was strong, his heart was lifted up to his destruction: for he transgressed against the Lord his God, and went into the temple of the Lord to burn incense upon the altar of incense." This was not his job. Uzziah was out of order. The priest warned him that it was the duty of the priest to light the incense in the sanctuary, but Uzziah believing in himself to be a great man disobeyed the priest and did as he personally wished. He became a proud man. Because of his actions, the Bible says immediately leprosy came upon his forehead and he died a leper. Anytime that we knowingly disobey God and commit transgression our hearts have become lifted up to destruction. Pride is dangerous!

Gifts and callings are without repentance. The gifts, the talents, and the calling God has bestowed us is ours eternally. God gives each of us a will. What we do with the gifts, the talents and the callings is strictly up to us - our will. Notice, if they are not used for the glory of God, our talents are without any anointing: useless and temporary. They add nothing to the Kingdom of God, so their livelihood is limited. It is the anointing that destroys the yoke. You are anointed to do the work for God and you must not take that anointing lightly. God has to place his anointing on your talent and your calling to be effective.

When He has so graciously forgiven us and excelled our gifts, we must be careful where the glory and praise takes place: in our heart and not in our head. If in our head, then we become controlled by our emotions and can get caught up in the hype. We become unbalanced. Consequently, we are destined to fall. Our sense of truth becomes warped because we are ignoring the source of our anointing. Always acknowledge Him!

On the other hand, if praise and glory is in our heart, we will know that we are blessed because of the mercies of God and nothing less. We have what we have because of God. We can do what we do because of God. We are who we are because of God. When we refer to the heart, it is not the organ that pumps blood; but rather it is our mind, our intellect, the area where reasoning takes place. That is why the scripture says to let this mind be in you which is also in Christ Jesus that you may have a compassionate heart of flesh and not of stone. Stony hearts do not receive God as the ultimate giver of gifts. They don't glorify God, but rather glorify themselves. The glory belongs to God. All that I am and all that I hope to be is in God!

Nothing is too hard for God. He can change the stony heart of anyone to a heart of flesh. A heart of flesh represents one of kindness and understanding. Perhaps you are involved with someone who appears to have a heart of stone. This can be changed. "And I will give them one heart, and I will put a new spirit within you; and I will take the stony heart out of their flesh, and will give them a heart of flesh" (Ezekiel 11:19). Try replacing the word 'them', 'you' and the word 'their' with the name of that person in the scripture, "And I will give Tom one heart ...." With constant confession and prayer watch the heart change!

Entertainers in the secular world are blessed with strong gifts of singing, dancing, acting, etc. God leaves it up to them how they use the gifts. When award time rolls around, many who receive the Emmy, the Oscar, etc., will begin their acknowledgements with, "I want to thank God, my grandmother and my mother." We have to give them credit for at least acknowledging God. There are those who just thank the Academy and their fans with no reference to their Creator. How sad this is. We should acknowledge Him in all our ways and He promised to direct our path. "This book of the law shall not depart out of thy mouth; but thou shalt meditate therein day and night, that thou mayest observe to do according to all that is written therein: for then thou shat make thy way prosperous, and then thou shalt have good success" (Joshua 1:8). You don't know true success until you know God!

Pride: Let it go!

Chapter X

FEAR

Let it go......

It has been said that fear is the absence of faith. I would like to add to that definition. Fear is also the lack of knowledge. Knowledge is strength. Strength is confidence. The more knowledge you have of a subject, the more strength you gain. The more strength you have in any given area, the more confident you are in accessing a situation to become the victor as opposed to succumbing to being the victim. Without information, good decisions cannot be made. It is human nature to be afraid of the unfamiliar. Once knowledge is obtained, rational decisions can be made and fear is released.

-Fear-

Fear is paralyzing. It stunts abilities and growth. Ever been or seen a situation where you or someone else was so frightened that they screamed, but no sound was heard? The fear itself was paralyzing. Generally this is a fear of the unknown. You can't see what is behind you. You may not be aware of the environment or just not sure of what to expect. So fear takes over. The sure way to eliminate fear of something is to learn all you can about it. You should go into a state of affairs fully aware of what is taking place. GI Joe says that "knowing is half the battle." The enemy attacks us because he knows that we are unfamiliar with our authority, with our privileges, and with our power as Christians.

In the fall of 2007, I had tendon repair surgery on my left ankle. The surgeon had to actually scrape calcium build-up that had attached itself to my heel. My Achilles tendon had to be reunited with my heel. Trust me: this was not a pleasant experience. The day after the surgery, I was taken to the physical therapy room for instructions on how to maneuver without my ill foot hitting the ground. For six weeks, I was not to put any weight on the heel that had been repaired. I had six weeks in a hard cast, followed by six weeks in an immobilizer boot. The cast was very heavy and cumbersome. My first lesson was on the use of the wheel chair - how to turn and how to brake. This was easy. I learned to roll forward, backward and in a circle. No problem. The difficult part was when I had to stand and to use either crutches or a walker.

Using crutches was a little harder than I had anticipated. Seeing other people do it was much different from actually doing it myself. It is a learned process that didn't register with me. So, I opted for the walker. It was easier. The crutches gave me three legs to work with, but the walker actually gave me five. I had to hold on to the walker and hop with my good leg, never allowing my bad foot to hit the floor. This still was not easy, but easier than the crutches. No problem.

Because I live in a two-story home and all of my bedrooms are upstairs, the physical therapist had to show me how to maneuver up and down the stairs. His first instruction was to hold on to the banister with both hands close together and hop up the stairs one step at a time. The left arm actually crossed over the body to hold on to the railing. He had a prop for me to practice this technique. For me, this was easier said than done. To anyone who has the use of both feet and both legs, this sounds effortless. But when you are using just one leg and one foot, all of the weight is held up by that one good foot. I grabbed the banister, but nothing moved. I told my foot to move. My mind was moving, but my body wasn't. I could not hop that one step. My mind could not grasp the possibility of my moving just that one step and not falling. I could not do it. I was paralyzed. The therapist and my husband kept urging me to take the one step - just one step. I was too afraid. My release from the hospital was dependent upon how well I did in therapy. I did not get the release. The therapist recommended that I repeat therapy the next day. It turned out to be a replica of the day before. My lack of knowledge led to my lack of confidence which led to my lack of strength, and consequently my fear!

My release from the hospital came the third day with orders for a therapist to come and work with me at my home. She came the fourth day of my ordeal. She rendered my banister too weak to use the cross over method. (Either it was too weak or I was too heavy!) Her suggestion was to sit and pull myself up the stairs in a backward motion. To descend, I could also sit and come down one step at a time. This worked for me. I had less fear sitting than standing. I was assured that the steps could hold my weight. At the top of the stairs, someone would have to be there to help me stand and use the walker. She suggested that I not try this feat when I was at home alone. In fact, she thought it was best not to be upstairs when no one was home but me. No problem.

I was sent home from the hospital with a wheel chair, a four-legged walker, and bedside commode. I was fine with everything except the portable 'setae.' The therapist had to convince me that I would need it. He was right. I used it in the bathtub to allow me to sit and take a shower. It was also much higher than my commodes and could be placed on top of my toilet seats. It had handles that I could grab and steady myself on one foot. It ended up being a big help. The only problem was that it was rather large and heavy.

Whenever I needed it moved from the toilet to the tub, my husband would do it for me. He was so patient with me. Thank you James!

A part of my growing up training was to be independent and to not depend or expect anyone to do anything for me. It was a lesson I learned well. I had asked my husband so many times to help me. He had carried that thing up and down the stairs from one room to another. I decided one day that I can do this. This was about one week after surgery. I was home alone and I needed the portable seat to be moved from the tub to the toilet. I looked at the portable and the distance between the tub and the toilet. I could do this. Let the fear go. I reached over grabbed the portable, lifted it up out of the tub (remember I am leaning on one leg; the other one is lifted up off of the floor) and gave it my best shot. I missed my aim. I lost my balance and ended up on the floor between the two fixtures with the portable on top of me. What am I to do? No one is home to help me, but God. After shaking for about 3 minutes, I had to make a decision. I prayed and asked for help. I did not know how I was going to get up. Finally, I pushed the portable off of me, straightened out my legs, turned on my stomach, scooted forward, rose up on my knees and used the bathroom counter to lift up myself. Wow! So much for moving the portable! I let it stay where it was.

What I did not realize at that exact moment was what I had learned! Knowledge is power. Though I diligently tried, I could not handle the portable balancing on one leg. The next time I attempted this feat, I sat in a chair, lifted the portable seat, rested it on the tub, then rested it on my knee and gradually turned which allowed me to successfully place the portable on top of the toilet without falling. The more I did this, the stronger I became with not only handling the portable, but with other taxing situations. Everyday was a learning experience of how I could handle things while being slightly incapacitated. It was a joy to discover what I could do on my own. The more knowledge I gained, the stronger I became, the more confident I was, and the more fears I released!

James 4:7 states, "Submit your selves therefore to God. Resist the devil and he will flee from you." We often quote the 'b' portion of that scripture with boldness, but we must never leave off the submitting of ourselves to God. We will never completely surrender to someone we do not know. We don't trust a candidate until we learn something about him. He won't get our vote and we won't surrender to his promises. We may say that we will, but in all actuality the surrender comes with trust. Trust comes with knowing to whom you must surrender. The more I study the Word of God, the more I know about God. The more I know about God, the more I trust Him. Every scripture gives me strength. The more I trust Him, the more I submit to His Will and to His Way.

Submitting to His will released my fear. Not my will God, but thy will be done. I trust in God; He cares for me. Oh that I may know

Him in the power of his resurrection and the fellowship of his suffering!

Studying the Bible releases fear. It teaches us by example the privileges that we have as Christians. From the beginning, God delegated man over the fish of the sea, the fowl in the air, and every living creature that creepeth upon the face of the earth. It stands to reason that if we have dominion over something, we should not fear it. We are in charge. Only when we "let them see our sweat" does our dominion power diminish. It has been said that a dog can sense your fear. We can never let a dog know that we are afraid. If he smells our fear, he will taunt us at his will.

God did not give us the spirit of fear, but of love, power and a sound mind. Love should replace fear. Let's look at the **Influence of LOVE**.

Love *COVERETH* all sins – *II Samuel 1:26*

"I am distressed for thee, my brother Jonathan: very pleasant hast thou been unto me: thy love to me was wonderful, passing the love of women."

Love is a *BANNER* over us – Song of Solomon 2:4

"He brought me to the banqueting house, and his banner over me was love."

Love is *STRONG* as death – Song of Solomon 8:7

"Now therefore, behold, the Lord bringeth up upon them the waters of the river, strong and many even the king of Assyria, and his glory; and he shall coup up over all his channels and go over all his banks."

Love *WORKETH* no ill – Romans 13:10

"Love worketh no ill to his neighbor: therefore love is the fulfilling of the law."

Love *IS* God – I John 4:7

"Beloved, let us love one another: for love is of God; and every one that loveth is born of God, and knoweth God."

There is *NO FEAR* in love – I John 4:18

"There is no fear in love; but perfect love casteth out fear: because fear hath torment. He that feareth is not made perfect in love." If I have love what is there to fear?

God said that we have power and we have dominion. Now we will examine the Power of Love.

He has given power to men – Matthew 9:8

"But when the multitudes saw it, they marveled and glorified God, which had given power unto men."

We have power to get wealth – Deuteronomy 8:18

"But thou shalt remember the Lord thy God: for it is he that giveth the power to get wealth..."

Christ promised us power

Isaiah 40:29 - "He giveth power to the faint; and to them that have no might he increaseth strength."

We have the power to become the sons of God

John 1:12 "...But as many as received him, to them gave he power to become the sons of God, even to them that believe on his name."

Mark 16:16-18 describes our power best

"He that believeth and is baptized shall be saved, but he that believeth not shall be damned. And these signs shall follow them that believe, in my name shall they cast our devils; they shall speak with new tongues; they shall take up serpents; and if they drink any deadly thing, it shall not hurt them: they shall lay hands on the sick and they shall recover." What power God has given unto man!

It is up to us to utilize all of the power that God offers. If we were given a fully furnished house, how would we live in it? We were given the keys to every lock. We had access to each room to live in, eat and sleep. Would you just stop in the living room and not go into the dining room? Would you stop in the family room and not go into the kitchen? Would you visit the bathrooms and not check out the bedrooms? I think not. The Word of God is like unto this house. Why stop at part of the Word and not enjoy it all. God has already given us precious promises. He is a God that does not lie. He wants us to enjoy all aspects of righteous living.   Let go of the fear and enter into the joy of the Lord!

God will keep you in perfect peace whose mind is stayed on Him. There is an old cliché that I heard coming up as child in the church and did not quite figure what the elders were saying: "Lord, keep me in my right mind."   Living in an age when anything and everything we consume can be detrimental to our health, where daily we find out foods we have eaten for years are now giving us cancer, and where the air we breathe has been labeled unsafe, it is understandable that we are crazy with concern and half out of our minds! Peace of mind is essential to healthy living. If your mind is occupied with the cares of the world, it is considerably difficult to function. He has given us a sound mind. This basically means we pray instead of worry. If we choose to worry there is no need to pray.

Knowing the promises of God, of love, power and a sound mind, releases any fear that I have of the enemy. His word makes promises that I accept and apply. We should not be worried about what the enemy will do to us because God has promised that no weapon formed against us shall be able to prosper. Why fear, when you have God on your side.

Fear: Let it go!

Chapter XI

GRUDGES

Let it go...

What is a grudge? What is the purpose of a grudge? How long should we hold a grudge? Is it profitable to remain faithful to a family grudge? I submit to you that grudges are without purpose and are futile. They will not enhance your life one iota. I'm reminded of the bee that leaves his stinger in you and then goes on about its business. After delivering its sting it dies, but you are left with the pain. The person holding the grudge is enduring the pain and holding the bag of resentment while the one who delivered the sting is free to enjoy life with no baggage. Is it worth it?

By definition, according to Merriam-Webster, a grudge is "to be Unwilling to give or admit: give or allow reluctantly or resentfully."

-Grudges-

In other words, I will never admit that I was at fault. I blame you! Because you will not admit any wrong doing either, we are at a pivotal point in our relationship. When there is not one party willing to forgive or to acknowledge wrong doing, chaos is developed and the grudge begins. All of this could be avoided if only one person would be eager to give in to save the friendship. This is where satan sieges an opportunity. Why play into his hand? This is what he wants among the Saints. He wants to break the peace. Is it worth it?

Satan's tactic is to divide and conquer. He knows together we stand, but divided we fall. He knows that he can only win when we are divided. So, he makes us jealous of each other's talents and gifts. He makes us read the same thing and believe totally different. He separates us by manipulating God's doctrine. He encourages us to develop our own righteousness so that we can believe in your own way. Satan convinces us that a strong relationship with God is not necessary. So he makes us think that we are too tired to pray and that we have worked too hard to go to church. Satan knows that if he tears down relationships, he will have a better chance at destroying our families. His aim is the Church. However, he fails to realize the gates of hell cannot prevail against the Church!

Choosing not to forgive can be detrimental to both your physical as well as your spiritual health. It is mandated by God that we forgive.

"For if ye forgive men their trespasses, your heavenly Father will also forgive you: But if ye forgive not men their trespasses, neither will your Father forgive your trespasses" (Matthew 6:14 and 15). God says, 'I will if you will.' He is just to forgive us our sins, but yet we find difficulty in forgiving one another. If we are to be Christ-like, then we have to be that way in every sense of the word. "Who is a God like unto thee, that pardoneth iniquity, and passeth by the transgression of the remnant of his heritage? He retaineth not his anger forever, because he delighteth in mercy" (Micah 7:18). God is merciful toward us. He pardons our iniquities and passes by our transgressions. Who are we to hold a grudge? We have sinned against a holy God who desires to forgive us.

Love and grudge are on opposite ends of the spectrum. We cannot demonstrate true love and display bitterness toward our brother. Love is an emotion that matures. It may begin as puppy love that will not sustain, but it can end in real love that hides a multitude of faults. At some point in our lives, we should have graduated to a love that looks beyond another's actions or words and sees the spirit that lies beneath the sudden out burst.   God looks beyond our faults and He sees our needs. If God decided to hold us responsible for every sin; every abomination; every lie we told; every person we hurt; every grape we have stolen from the grocery store or every pen we took from work, He would have a grudge until the end of time. Instead He continuously shows us His grace and mercy. Let me remind you of a definition of grace and mercy.

-Grudges-

Grace is when we get what we don't deserve and mercy is when we don't get what we do deserve. God does not hold a grudge. He loves us in spite of ourselves!

Consequences of holding a grudge:

1) Anger festers
2) Tempers are lost
3) Resentment builds
4) Feelings are hurt
5) Friendships end
6) Relationships die
7) Love is replaced with hate
8) Understanding vanishes
9) Statements are made that we regret
10) Foolish behavior is exhibited.

Looking at this list of consequences, now the question becomes, "Is it worth it?" Count up the cost and you will see that holding a grudge is not worth the effort. It takes more energy to be angry than it does to smile and to find the solution to forgive. Isaiah wrote in his 2nd chapter, "Come now, and let us reason together, saith the Lord." What a brilliant idea: reason. There is an explanation for any action. The root of the problem needs to be examined. If there is an apparent attitude, why is this attitude present? What are the circumstances that caused the attitude? It is necessary for the opposing sides to agree to lay aside any of their differences, and come together for the good of the cause or for the length of the relationship. Find out why he or she said what was said or why that person acted a certain way. What was the reason? This should not be a problem for Christians. We are the ones who should be willing to give in when the sinners won't. "Blessed are the peacemakers: for they shall be called the children of God" (Matthew 5:9).

To be a peacemaker, we must have peace. Peace starts in the heart. Only God can give the type of peace that surpasses all understanding. Peace can be better than money because a person can be filthy rich and can't sleep at night. We look at entertainers who have great sums of money, but are never fulfilled. They go from one relationship to another, one drug to another, trying to experience fulfillment, but yet they remain unfulfilled. The void that they possess can only be filled by a relationship with the Peace Giver, the only potentate: Jesus Christ. Money does not complete you and neither does people or drugs. Christ says, "Peace I leave with you, my peace I give unto you: not as the world giveth, give I unto you. Let not your heart be troubled neither let it be afraid" (John 14:27).

Angry people are generally unhappy people for one reason or another because they have no peace. They are dissatisfied with their environment; hate the job; dislike the community where they live; unsatisfied with the church they attend; do not like the dog or the cat and are misunderstood by their peers. This kind of misery loves company. Because they are unhappy, they want the world to be unhappy as well. So they sow discord among the brethren. They are wishy-washy - double-minded and always stirring up something on the job. They inwardly want others to feel the way they do. They hold grudges so long that they forget how and with whom it originated.

The story of Jacob and Esau is the utmost example of a grudge relinquished in the Old Testament. Jacob and Esau were brothers - sons of Isaac. Jacob swindled Esau out of his birthright and his blessing. Esau's own greed and impatience caused him to give up his birthright to Jacob for a bowl of soup. Jacob and Rebecca (mother of the two sons), devised a plan that caused Esau to miss his blessing. Isaac was to give his blessing to the eldest son. Instead Jacob went in disguised as his brother, Esau, deceived their father, and received the blessing that was intended for the firstborn. When Esau finally went to his father for the blessing, it had already been given to Jacob. It could only be administered one time according to Jewish tradition. Esau had to leave with less than what he was entitled.

It had already been prophesied that the older child would serve the younger; therefore, no work was necessary on the part of the family members. Often when we take matters into our own hands, we make bad situations even worse. God wants us to wait on him.

"...They that wait upon the Lord shall renew their strength; they shall mount up with wings as eagles; they shall run and not be weary; they shall walk and not faint." Never get weary in your work for the Lord. It is not in vain! God has a plan.

Jacob's very name means trickster. After these episodes, he was told by his mother to flee the country for his life and journey to her brother's home; there he would find a wife. Jacob left knowing that his brother had set out to slay him. *What goes around comes around.* Jacob worked 7 years under his Uncle Laban for the woman of his dreams. But because she was the younger of two sisters, he was given the eldest daughter on his wedding night when he was too inebriated to tell the difference. In order to get the woman for which he had worked, Jacob had to commit to work another 7 years.

Many years passed and both brothers had established families with servants, livestock and cattle. Jacob, whose name had been changed by God to Israel, found himself in a situation where he had to confront his brother. Jacob feared for his life and that of his family. He arranged his family and servants in a manner such that the wife he loved the most, Rachel, would be in the back of the caravan. This was done just in case Esau had come to destroy them (Rachel would have time to flee). "And Esau ran to meet him, and embraced him, and fell on his neck, and kissed him: and they wept." The grudge was over. Esau had made up in his mind that it just was not worth it! Love does and should conquer all. We have to ask ourselves, "Is it worth it?"

Grudges: Let them go!

Chapter XII

THE CONCLUSION OF THE
MATTER

Let it go...

It has taken me many years to complete this project. I kept setting goal dates, but never reached them. Something *was* holding me back. There was something that I would not 'let go.' Issues in our lives are occasionally hidden. We may think that we have it all together, but there lies within a 'won't let go demon.' There is an inner questionable feeling, but we just can't put our finger on the problem. We move on without addressing the issue. When we allow it to fester, it grows to gigantic proportions. Our plans are thwarted and goals seem unattainable. It is up to us to make a decision to 'let go'. These unattained goals are played out in many scenarios. For example, battered women remain in precarious positions until they realize that what they are holding on to is not worth the torment: the abuse, both physical and mental.   A breakthrough is needed to be released from the control of the demon. A plan has to be put in place and carried out. A decision has to be made. With resolve, those of us who have had enough will make an affirmative decision.

Roman 12:2 states, "Be not conformed to this world, but be ye transformed by the renewing of your mind." To let go of abusive spouses, parents, children, relationships, possessions, pride, fear, grudges and yes diseases, we must make a decision. Our minds have to be renewed. If we keep thinking that we will get out of the rut someday and never work towards removing ourselves, we will go even lower than we could imagine. Let go of the past and look forward to the future. Engage in activities that cause hope and change. Be transformed from an old mind set of hatred, jealousy and worry. Be transformed into a new mind of love, joy and peace. Let go of the hurt and disgust and be renewed. Be renewed in your thinking and in your conversation. Remember the power of death and life is in the tongue!

Weigh the cost. Many things we hold on to are just not worth the trouble. Consider the loss. Ask this: "What will it cost me to grow and what decision will cause me to remain stagnant? Is it worth it?" Consider this scenario: Sis. Sukie is upset with me about something and I don't know what it is. I have gone to her and inquired of the problem. No viable answer was given. She still will not speak to me unless I speak first. She ignores me and goes the other way when she sees me coming. What do I do? Do I not speak to her and allow her to flunk my religion? Do I speak to her and keep walking? Try this: Continue to love and let it go. Continue to speak and let it go. Continue to pray and let it go! Time maybe the solution. Sis. Sukie needs time to heal and to mend from whatever issues she is fighting. Your job is to let it go with love.

Nothing is worth losing your integrity and hindering your relationship with God. He is the ultimate one to please. He gives the peace. Letting go of insignificant matters will leave you feeling free and spiritually healthy. Step out of bondage. The enemy's job is to keep you bound with trivial matters. He wants your relationships bound, your finances bound and your emotions bound. He is a deceiver. There is no truth in him because he is a liar. Take a stand against his wiles and let go of his strongholds. Live in freedom. Live in the newness of God. Make a decision that you will not allow satan to bind your thoughts or your actions. Never give way to his ploys. You are in charge of your destiny, not the devil. You make the final decision of whether to hold on to something or *to let it go.*

Letting go allows you to enter into true FREEDOM. It is good to consider and understand your past, but you cannot hold on to the insecure feelings it may cause. Just like being released from debt is an awesome feeling, so is being released from those areas that cause us pain. Forgiveness is the best virtue you can have. God has warned us that we must forgive others before He will forgive us. "Forgive us our debts as we forgive our debtors." Thank you, God, that we can live in the future accepting the past, but not holding on to it. Live in freedom. Live debt free!

Just Let It Go!

MAMA

The Final Chapter

On January 4, 2011 I realized the reason this book took as long as it did to complete. The last chapter had never spiritually manifested. Therefore, it could not be written. This was the day that my sibling and I buried the Matriarch of our family. We had held on to Mama for as long as we could. We finally made a unanimous decision to "let her go".

Mama had been slowly deteriorating with Alzheimer's since 2002. It was a dawdling decline; inevitable, but denied by my family. We had to come to grips with the fact that she would never be the same. When do you separate hope for inevitability? How do you determine God's will? Never give up hope. Nothing is inevitable when you have faith in God. You will never know God's will. His thoughts are far above ours as the east is from the west and the north is from the south.

At best, we accept what God allows. We trust Him. It was as painful the day she died as it was for anyone loosing a loved one, but it was a circumstance that we could not change. I'm not sure that we would want to make a change. Mama would not want to return to the pain and suffering. She would not want an extended burden on her children. God knows what He is doing and this was a way out that we could comprehend. Mama was tired. She had

-Mama-

reared four children; witnessed the birth of 11 grand children and experienced a wonderful marriage of 57 years. She knew God and He knew her. If she could have spoken at the final hour I am sure that she would have said, "Let me go."

APPENDIX ONE

7 Things to Never Let Go

1) Your Relationship with God

"Who shall separate us from the love of Christ? Shall tribulation, or distress, or nakedness, or peril, or sword? As it is written, for thy sake we are killed all the day long; we are accounted as sheep for the slaughter. Nay, in all these things we are more than conquerors through him that loved us. For I am persuaded, that neither death, nor life, nor angels, nor principalities, nor powers, or thing present, no thing to come, nor height, no depth, nor any other creature shall be able to separate us from the love of God, whish is in Christ Jesus our Lord." Romans 8:35-39

2) Your Dreams

"And the Lord answered me and said, Write the vision, and make it plain upon tables, that he may run that readeth it. For the vision is yet for an appointed time, but as the end it shall speak and not lie; though it tarry, wait for it; because it will surely come, it will not tarry." Habakkuk 2:2-3

3) Your Compassion

"Finally, be ye all of one mind having compassion one of another, love as brethren, be pitiful, be courteous; Nor rendering evil for evil, or railing for railing: but contrariwise blessing, knowing that ye are thereunto called, that ye should inherit a blessing." I Peter 3:8-9

4) Your Hope

"That by two immutable things, in which it was impossible for God to lie, we might have a strong consolation, who have fled for refuge to lay hold upon the hope set before us: Which hope we have as an anchor of the soul, both sure and steadfast, and which entereth into that within the veil." Hebrews 6:18-19

5) Your Faith

"Moreover it is required in stewards that a man be found faithful." I Corinthians 4:2 "Fear none of those things which thou shalt suffer; behold, the devil shall cast some of you in prison, that ye may be tried, and ye shall have tribulation ten days; be thou faithful unto death, and I will give thee a crown of life." Revelation 2:10

6) Your Desire to Learn

"Come unto me, all ye that labor and are heavy laden, and I will give you rest. Take my yoke upon you, and learn of me; for I am meek and lowly in heart: and ye shall find rest unto your souls. For my yoke is easy and my burden is light." Matthew 11:28-30

7) Your Willingness to Change

"But we all, with open face beholding as in a glass the glory of the Lord, are changed into the same image from glory to glory, even as by the Spirit of the Lord." II Corinthians 3:18

APPENDIX TWO

7 Things to Let Go

1) **Grudges**

"For if ye forgive men their trespasses, your heavenly Father will also forgive you. But if ye forgive not men their trespasses, neither will your Father forgive your trespasses." St Matthew 6:14,15

2) **Fear**

"There is no fear in love; but perfect love casteth out fear: because fear hath torment. He that feareth is not made perfect in love." I John 4:18

3) **Pride**

"When pride cometh, then cometh shame: but with the lowly is wisdom." Proverbs 11:2

4) **Possessions**

"For what is a man profited, if he shall gain the whole world, and lose his own soul? Or what shall a man give in exchange for his soul?" St Matthew 16:26

5) Unhealthy Relationships

"But Jesus said unto him, Follow me; and let the dead bury their dead." St. Matthew 8:22

6) Religion as oppose to Relationship

"Brethren, my heart's desire and prayer to God for Israel is, that hey might be saved. For I bear them record that they have a zeal of God, but not according to knowledge. For they being ignorant of God's righteousness and going about to establish their own righteousness, have not submitted themselves unto the righteousness of God. Romans 10:1-3

7) Loved Ones Who Have Moved On

"The righteous perisheth, and no man layeth it to heart: and merciful men are taken away, none considering that the righteous is taken away from the evil to come. Isaiah 57:1

Jude 24-26

Now unto Him

That is able to keep you from falling,

And to present you faultless

Before the presence of His Glory

With exceeding joy,

To the only wise God our Savior,

Be glory and majesty,

Dominion and power

Both now and ever.

Amen!

ABOUT THE BOOK

Life is all about choices. The goal of this book is to help readers consider certain options before making final choices in life. No one can make choices for us. Any final decision is ours, but we must be willing to let go of disturbing baggage before going forward.

This book is about releasing all unto God, looking to Him who is the Author and Finisher of our faith. It took several years to complete this project. I had situations and people that I was holding on to for dear life. However, God demanded my allegiance. He demands total allegiance from all of us. When there are situations that should not be present in our lives, He warns us. Yet, we ignore warnings that could keep us safe and keep us in a growing relationship with Him.

God's love for us is enduring. He allows us time to get our acts together and to walk in His will, but still we must let go of the baggage. We need to release those feelings, emotions, and even people who are hindering our walk with God.

Each word of paragraph in this book is backed by the Word of God and the Holy Ghost.

May you find comfort in knowing the situations, the circumstances, issues and problems that you release unto God are well in the Keeper's Care!

About The Author

Gladys Kepney White

is the founder and president of FAVOR Ministries, Incorporated in Mobile, Alabama. Overseer White is thrice ordained with an increasing thirst for God's work and His Word. She is a lover of people and devotes time and energy to helping others reach their full potential. She is a wife, mother of three adult children with four grandchildren.

Her first book, "A Safe Place for Mama" stemmed from a desire to make aware the challenges families endure when faced with a loved one stricken with Alzheimer's. The book is written in a light hearted structure, but full of insight on handling a devastating disease. "When to Let Go" is a flowing sequel to "A Safe Place" for Mama. It is an addendum to what has already been written.

Overseer White's desire is that you are challenged and inspired as you read this book to consider letting go of negative relationships as you move forward in your walk with God!

9 780615 586083